Be a Real-Life MERMAID

Unleash Your Inner Siren
with a Colorful Swimmable Tail,
Seashell Jewelry and Decor,
Glamorous Hair and Makeup,
Fin-tastic Persona and More

VIRGINIA HANKINS

Ulysses Press

Published in the U.S. by
Ulysses Press
P.O. Box 3440
Berkeley, CA 94703
www.ulyssespress.com

ISBN: 978-1-61243-712-5
Library of Congress Control Number: 2017937993

Printed in the United States by Bang Printing
10 9 8 7 6 5 4 3 2 1

Acquisitions editor: Bridget Thoreson
Managing editor: Claire Chun
Editor: Renee Rutledge
Design and layout: Malea Clark-Nicholson
Photographs: © Virginia Hankins except mermaid photos (pages 4, 6, 9, 17, 41, 45, 69, 71, 72, 74, 80, 103, 125, and 127) © Brenda Stumpf; Shell-ebration Beach Waves (pages 47–50) © Cheryl Hankins
Models: Esteela Boedeker, Virginia Hankins, Alissa Quon, Kaia Stachel-Zambryski
Artwork: scale pattern © RRA79/shutterstock.com

Distributed by Publishers Group West

CONTENTS

NOTE FROM THE AUTHOR

"Darling it's better,
down where it's wetter,
take it from me."

—SEBASTIAN THE CRAB

Hello, and welcome to my world! I heard that you were curious as to how to be a mermaid, and I can't wait to help. I'm known in the industry as Catalina Mermaid, a bona fide pro-fishional, as we pros jokingly call it. I'm a genuine professional mermaid, an underwater safety and stunt coach who helps people just like you to celebrate their world and lead more fin-tastic lives. In this book, I'll be your tour guide/mermaid master coach for diving in to this truly amazing world.

First off, I have a secret for you. Before a person is born, they are, at first, a mermaid. You see, until birth a person essentially lives as a mermaid, surviving in a liquid environment, a world of darkness and muted sound, where legs don't matter and gravity is a lesser necessity. It's only upon birth that mermaids become humans by being thrust into a foreign land of light, noise, and dryness, forced to get around on those two strange things...what do you call them? Oh, feet, also known as "those things you trip over on land."

You may have been one of those kids watching mermaid movies and daydreaming about towering kelp forests, talking crabs, clown fish, and surging turquoise waves along sun-drenched beaches. You may have been the girl in school with the pink glitter dolphins everywhere or the guy who simply would not stop jumping off the roof into the backyard pool (to the justifiable horror of his parents). Regardless of who you are, part of you knows that the adventure of the water is calling you, and you want to go see it for yourself.

That's what this book is all about—honing in on that dream and helping you swim right in to a metaphorical riptide to a more fin-tastic life. So, are you ready? Let's go!

THE MERMAID PHILOSOPHY

For as long as humans have been living near water, they have been creating stories and traditions. Stories, now more than ever before, keep us engaged and interested in the world, sharing our similarities across oceans and borders to remind us that all people are tied to water.

One of my favorite stories growing up was called "The Queen of Tung Ting Lake," from a children's storybook of Chinese fairy tales. It's similar to many ancient mermaid lore pieces where a mermaid can shape shift into the form of an aquatic animal, such as a seal, fish, dolphin, or snake. In the story, a poor, struggling man named Chen watches his commanding officer spear a seal for fun and drag it on board the sailing vessel that they are riding on. In an act of empathy, when Chen realizes that the officer isn't interested in actually eating, skinning, or otherwise using the injured seal, he performs first aid on the animal and returns it to the lake. The seal gleefully barks its delight and is greeted in joy by a school of swirling fish before swimming away.

The days pass, the seal is forgotten, and Chen takes a new trip one year later. One day, a massive, thrashing storm sinks the boat that Chen is riding on and throws him into the lake's tumultuous waters. By some miracle, he is able to escape the fate of drowning by clinging to a floating basket until he washes up on the shore. When he is strong enough to explore, he discovers an entire hidden land ruled by women, where art, nature, and sport are championed in daily life and a shape-shifting queen presides over life and death.

Fortunately for Chen, the princess, a beautiful young woman with the remarkable ability to change herself into a fish, recognizes him. She introduces him to the queen (who is able to transform herself into the seal he had saved before), and the queen repays his previous kindness by not only giving him a pardon on his life, but also entrusting him with her daughter in marriage and a fabulous amount of riches, all out of regard for him being a person of empathy and character who respected an animal of the water.

Of all the mermaid stories that I have read, "The Queen of Tung Ting Lake" seems to have the most relevance to the modern mermaid philosophy of standing up for what you know is right. Being a modern mermaid or merman, you may not have the magical ability to shape-shift into a fish or seal, but you can live a form of higher life that is enriched by beauty, joy, strength, empathy, and adventure wherever you happen to live. Here are things that you can do to start.

ADVENTURE RESPONSIBLY

Like Chen, you have the ability to enjoy the natural world without harming it. No one person owns the world, nor will any person own the things in the world forever. Instead, each person has a duty to help preserve and protect it so that future generations of people, animals, and plants may also have a good home. Instead of going to a movie theater or shopping mall, develop a commitment to your physical and psychological fitness by going to a local park for your nature fix. Consider donating money to the local park, and while you are in there, take the time to recycle or throw away litter responsibly, regardless of if it is yours. Stay on marked trails to avoid trampling over delicate plants and, if going in the water, be aware of where you place your feet so that you don't kill tide pool animals or fragile coral structures.

REFLECT ON USE

While you might not be faced with a live seal in your decisions, you can choose to put your "seal" of approval on your buying choices by thinking them through. As an example, consider investing in a reusable aluminum water bottle rather than buying crates of disposable plastic water bottles. Simply carrying your own reusable water bottle with you and refilling it from clean tap water can pay for its up-front cost in a few weeks. According to ReusethisBag.com, bringing your own reusable shopping bag can keep between 350 and 500 disposable plastic bags out of landfills in a single year. Skipping the straw and the plastic takeout bag at a fast food restaurant can save two pieces of single-use trash from ever being used. Opting for BPA-free reusable containers while cooking at home keeps deforestation from cardboard boxes down and keeps plastic zip-top bags away from landfills too.

SWIM WITH THE CURRENT

The ocean is one of the most dynamic ecosystems in the world. Its tides, waves, and currents constantly change to adapt to variables. As a result, the ocean is one of the most unpredictable yet alluring environments to experience. The wise mermaid or merman knows to swim with the ocean and remain flexible in their approach to life to be able to work in harmony with the energy around them and ride a wave of success when the timing is right.

LEND A FIN

Like the mermaid immortalized in Hans Christian Andersen's famous tale, *The Little Mermaid*, the nature of modern mermaids is to be courteous and helpful ambassadors to the world. By bringing others joy while maintaining healthy boundaries, a mermaid or merman can experience the fulfillment of meeting new friends, sharing mutual interests, and creating their own happiness.

Consider creating opportunities for people to gather and enjoy themselves. Provide a welcome home to guests, and seek to enhance your world by taking time to add beauty to it. You can be a person of worth by simply being honest, respectful, considerate, kind, and dedicated to a lifetime of learning.

SHOW YOUR BEST SELF

To be successful in any endeavor is to live in pursuit of excellence that is honed from hours of dedication, hard work, and passion. The most successful people in the world *never* stop learning. They are always working toward excellence and are keenly aware that to be good at what they do, they must both take time to enrich their minds and bodies, for without health, dreams are unattainable, and without dreams, a body is never used to its fullest potential. If you start to doubt yourself, stop and remember that everyone in the world had to learn their talent sometime. The fact that you may feel inadequate, behind, or bad at something is

only a self-issued judgment on your current situation. You don't need to believe it. Acknowledge it, see yourself correctly as a person who is learning, and keep working on your goal. This dedication is the ultimate key to your success.

SWIM WITH SELF-RELIANCE

In any industry, you can always tell who the true pro-fishionals are. They are on time, prepared, cheerful, courteous, and self-reliant. When difficulties arise, they offer suggestions based on real experience with consideration for the egos of others. They have a heightened understanding of where they are needed and are polite yet transparent about what they can and cannot do. They realize that their safety and that of those around them depend on their commitment to perform their hard-earned skills to the best of their ability. "Show time" means demonstrating their past practice, not the hope of "getting it right this time." In business or in life, just as in swimming, if you lack the skills needed to do your job or fail to do them, you drown. When you know that you can trust your own skills and judgment, you become powerful because you have found your own proven truth. You will cease to care what Internet trolls think of you, stop placing others' expectations above your own happiness, and emerge in a place where your inner voice matters far more to you than trying to be someone else's ideal. Think again of *The Little Mermaid* (this time the Disney version). Ariel didn't need to vocalize her thoughts publicly because she trusted her own instincts and knew that she not only had the swimming skills to save the prince, but also to win him over when others would have passed her by.

SWIM WITH THE SHARKS

Each one of us needs to learn to swim with the sharks, or face our own fears, whether than means going up against more accomplished competitors in a contest, applying for new jobs, or trying new experiences. Swimming with sharks can be scary. The good news is that Franklin D. Roosevelt was right: "The only thing we have to fear is fear itself." Once you face them up close, the sharks look much less intimidating.

How will you start to live a fin-tastic life? Construct your own ideas for action in the table below.

CONCEPT	ACTION
Adventure Responsibly	
Reflect on Use	
Swim with the Current	
Lend a Fin	
Show Your Best Self	
Swim with Self-Reliance	
Swim with the Sharks	

MERMAID MAKEOVER

When embarking on a fun journey to become a real mermaid, it can be helpful to think about what type of water creature you are. Once you have a character in mind, it is simple to tie in colors and accents to suit that character. We call that "developing a mer-sona."

WHAT KIND OF MER-SONALITY DO YOU HAVE?

Use your gut instinct to quickly answer "a" or "b" in each of the questions below.

1. You have the most in common with
   a. Sharks. You're not someone that everyone understands, but those who do adore you.
   b. Dolphins. You love playing and coming up with creative new ideas.
2. A perfect day for you is
   a. Exploring the wide-open sea
   b. Relaxing on your favorite beach
3. Children are
   a. Obnoxious
   b. Adorable
4. Can you sing?
   a. Yes
   b. No…well, maybe
5. Which phrase do you best agree with?
   a. Don't put all your eggs in one basket.
   b. If you can believe it, you can achieve it.
6. You prefer
   a. To work by yourself
   b. To work in a group
7. If you saw a person you really didn't like drowning, you would
   a. Help
   b. Get help
8. You would rather
   a. Live in a sheltered grotto surrounded by caves, moss, and waterfalls
   b. Live in a sunken ship with lots of relics to play with
9. If you could choose one ocean animal as a pet, it would be
   a. An octopus. It is clever and unique.
   b. A cow-nosed ray. It is always curious and smiling.

If you chose mostly As, congratulations, you're a SIREN!

Complex, introspective, clever, and adventurous, sirens have traditionally had a bad reputation for sinking ships, drowning sailors, and well, getting their way. They started out as half-bird, half-women back when Odysseus was sailing around getting lost, and have gradually evolved into the sexual and stunning she-wolf packs of the seas as seen in *Pirates of the Caribbean*. I'm sure that male sirens exist; they just tend to keep to their own counsel and lead a much less public life outside of West Hollywood gay bars. Part of the charm of these hauntingly charismatic water dwellers is that sirens get what they want. Rather than living by the rules of society, a siren creates his or her own rules. When on your adventures, be sure to take some time to be by yourself to recharge and think about how you are going to approach your day. Meditation is an amazing pastime for sirens, as is organizing a skull collection, studying piranhas, and plotting to take over the world.

If you chose mostly Bs, congratulations, you're a MERMAID!

Bubbly, social, and full of good cheer, you can hear a mermaid coming before you see her. She always seems to be surrounded by people, waves, and lots of noise. Mermaids view life as a treasure chest half-full, loaded with interesting, sparkling things that can sometimes hold their brief attention span. And then again, maybe not. While they tend to be less organized and less together overall than sirens, for some reason you can't help but like them. And, if you don't, they'll probably win you over. These lovable water dwellers are sure to make you smile.

★★★

Do you feel like neither of these is quite you? If so, then you might be one of these other fascinating water dwellers.

RUSALKA. Eerie, deadly, emotionally disturbed, and highly territorial, you know you have met a rusalka when a random young woman tries to drown you in a local freshwater river or pond. These poor Pisces really can't help it. You see, they were scorned so badly in their love lives that they could only escape their own horrible sorrow by drowning themselves. It isn't quite clear if now they are seeking revenge or just want to throw an underwater tea party with a new companion, but either way, it's best to steer clear!

SELKIE. Selkies are from Great Britain and have the powerful ability to shape-shift into seals for truly superior swimming ability. When it gets too cold, this water-loving being can simply shed its skin and walk onto land in human form to, say, grab some fish and chips without having to personally hunt for it, or melt the heart of a hot lifeguard. Realistically, being a selkie would seem to be the ultimate answer to being where the people are while also living down where it's wetter—except for one vulnerability. Their seal pelt has to be hidden well when they are on land for, if it were found by a human and hidden, they would have to stay in seal form and with that person, which could be awkward, for example, if that person were a seal hunter or a fan of wearing fur.

CHOOSING A NAME

To be a true star fish, you need to be unique in who you are. Every good mermaid or merman character starts with a few key things: a name, home location, mer-sonality type, and backstory. A backstory is a lot like a personal history; it explains who you are, where you came from, and some unique things about the way you approach the world that makes you stand out.

A one-of-a-kind mermaid or merman name is one of the most important things that you can think of and can be overwhelming with so many fin-tastic choices out there. This table makes it easy to create one if you are stuck. For example, if your given name is Andrea and you were born in July, then your name would be Mermaid Aqua of the Arctic Ocean.

THE FIRST LETTER OF YOUR FIRST NAME	YOUR MERMAID NAME	YOUR BIRTHDAY MONTH	YOUR LOCATION OF ORIGIN
A	Aqua	January	Pacific Ocean
B	Bubbles	February	Atlantic Ocean
C	Coral	March	Indian Ocean
D	Destiny	April	South China Sea
E	Enchancia	May	Caribbean Sea
F	Fin	June	Red Sea
G	Glitter	July	Arctic Ocean
H	Heron	August	Antarctic Ocean
I	Indigo	September	Mediterranean Sea
J	Jewel	October	Black Sea
K	Kelsea	November	Nile River
L	Lapis	December	Amazon River
M	Meridian		
N	Nixie		
O	Oceana		

P/Q	Pearl		
R	Riptide		
S	Shell		
T	Tide		
U	Undine		
V	Voyager		
W	Watersong		
X/Y/Z	Zephyr		

DESIGNING YOUR CHARACTER BACKSTORY

Think about the home location that you discovered in the prior table. What does it look like? What kinds of animals live there? Is it a hot environment or a cold environment? Is the water quiet and gentle or harsh and aggressive?

Based on the look of the location, think harder still. If you were a mermaid or a merman living at the location, realistically, what types of things would be at your disposal to use as tools, build into shelter, or hunt/gather for food? Often, an environment shapes its residents. A mermaid in the Hawaiian Islands of the Pacific Ocean may be able to create rope or lacing out of vines and construct it with dried coconut shells to make a custom-fit bra, while a mermaid living in a kelp forest full of large, leafy kelp could use that instead for cover. A merman living in the Indian Ocean might be influenced by the local custom of henna and delight in wearing unique stain designs that stay on underwater, while a merman living in the icy waters of the Arctic might scavenge for old narwhal tusks to use as a weapon in battle against hungry polar bears fighting for seal meat.

Once you know where you are from, what type of home you live in, and what types of tools or influences you have, it becomes easier to add in some other mer-sonality traits. Building on your assignment of siren or mermaid, think about how your personality could be shaped by the environment in which you live. Again, if you were a mermaid of the icy Arctic, perhaps, in order to warm yourself, you'd have to charm humans working in the area by telling stories, but if you were a siren of the Arctic, you would need to find a way to camouflage yourself against the white ice sheets to stay unseen from humans who would be interested in competing with you for prey.

Use this table to flesh out your mer-sonality and give some thought to your own unique character.

QUESTION	ANSWER
My name is:	
I am from:	
I am a (siren/mermaid):	
My home is special. It looks like:	
I do/do not have a pet. It is a:	
Something that I wear to remind me of my home or my favorite adventure is:	
I do/do not have a favorite food. It is:	
My favorite adventure was:	
My favorite thing to do is:	

MAKEUP FOR THE WATER & BEYOND

Modern mer-makeup comes in a daunting array of waterproof options. But are they really waterproof, as in they won't make you look like you had a bad date with a squid? Well, no. They aren't. There are, however, some brands that wear well and a few insider tips that can help you keep the ink in place so you can emerge from the water with a gorgeous face.

Sun Protection

The most important step in maintaining your beachy beauty is keeping hydrated by drinking lots of water and preventing health issues. Moisturizer is typically great for skin, but its oily properties can cause your "waterproof" makeup to melt away faster than Frosty the Snowman on a hot summer's day. Instead of moisturizing with an oil-based product, go light on the days you're in the water and opt for a powerful UVA/UVB sunscreen after thoroughly washing and drying your face instead.

Why sunscreen? Here's the reality. When you are a mermaid, you are out in the sun more than most other people. That means that you are more likely to be at risk for melanoma, a common form of cancer that actually kills one person in the world every hour. One UK study found that about 86 percent of melanomas can be attributed to exposure to ultraviolet (UV) radiation from the sun, and more sun means more risk. Thankfully, there is prevention available to that is cheap and portable. Layer up in the forms of 3-inch-wide brimmed hats, UV protective rash guards and swim clothing, polarized UVA-protective sunglasses, and sunscreen. Avoid being in the sun during peak daylight hours, between 10 a.m. and 4 p.m., if possible, and for goodness' sake, don't use tanning beds or tanning oils.

While things like wide-brimmed hats and sunglasses are fairly common and interchangeable in effectiveness, after four years of testing out just about every drugstore brand of waterproof sunscreen on the market, there is one clear winner for being the best sunscreen for mermaids and ocean enthusiasts: Ocean Potion. Not only does this brand have a tidally awesome name and come in big sizes at cheaper prices than more well-known brands, it *works*. After a full day playing in the sun in Honduras or Hawaii with minimal reapplications, the SPF 50 broad spectrum lotion keeps even redheads the right color. This brand is also both UVA and UVB spectrum protective. While most people know that UVB rays can cause skin coloring and sunburn, UVA rays may actually be the cause of wrinkles and skin cancer. Sunblocks that are broad spectrum and cover both UVA and UVB can help to better protect your skin from the invisible threats from sunlight.

So, do you know the proper way to apply that extra barrier against the sunlight? According to the Skin Cancer Foundation (www.skincancer.org), you should apply 1 ounce (2 tablespoons) of sunscreen to your entire body 30 minutes before going outside. They also recommend reapplying sunscreen every two hours or immediately after swimming or excessive sweating. The time before going outside helps to let the sunscreen dry so that it won't just wash off. A word of caution is to avoid getting sunscreen close to your eyes, as it may run and cause an uncomfortable burning sensation (particularly with more common drugstore brands). Use polarized sunglasses that block UVA to help with that area instead.

When you are done swimming, it is highly advised to immediately dry off and cover up with a hat, sunglasses, and lightweight or temperature-appropriate clothing to help your body get cover from the sun's rays. If you opt to swim more later, remember to reapply your sunblock.

Primer

After you have applied your sunblock and allowed it to dry, it's time to add a silicone-based primer (e.g., something containing an ingredient like dimethicone). Silicone-based primers, such as Urban Decay's Eyeshadow Primer Potion, help to prevent makeup creasing and smooth out the appearance of skin while giving other layers of makeup something to stick on to. You should have one primer specifically for your eyeshadow area and another for your face.

When you work with primers, a little can go a long way. Start by dotting some of it in the middle of your face and gently rub it in using your fingers toward the outer areas of the face. You will likely only need about a raisin-sized amount.

Let the primer set for a few minutes before applying foundation.

Color Corrector

Set the stage for a better complexion by using color correctors, if needed. Fair-skinned fish may find that a pale pink works the best for them in canceling out dark circles under the eyes, while medium-toned mermaids are better with a peach color corrector, and dark-skinned damselfish can benefit from the more orange tones of dark peach.

In general, greens cancel out redness, such as acne or skin irritation from chlorine, while lavender tones can help to cancel out yellow hues. A little goes a long way with color correctors, so be sure to start small and gradually add more with the tip of a finger to avoid looking like a patchwork quilt.

Foundation

The best of the drugstore foundation brands for water workers appears to be Revlon's ColorStay foundation. As long as you don't excessively wipe your face on your hands, towels, or other things, this clingy foundation is buildable, meaning that you can layer on additional foundation after each layer dries for a more opaque finish.

Apply foundation by starting at the middle of your face and blending outward. You can use a foundation brush for the main application and then blend by gently rolling a sponge beauty blender (or similar) tool over your foundation. Blend any excess foundation onto your ears and neck to ensure a natural look.

Concealer

If, after both correctors and foundation, you still see bumps, discolorations, or other unsightly skin effects, use a concealer to hide them.

Base Layer

At this point it's a good idea to set your base layer. Apply a light spray of Ben Nye's Final Seal to your face and let it dry. Pro-fishional mermaids swear by this product for its reliable results and easy-to-use spray.

Blush

Add more color to your face with something like Dream Bouncy Blush by Maybelline, a cream-style blush that repels water. The consistency takes some getting used to but once you do, it has nice staying power with an easy fingertip application. Remember that underwater colors will appear to be more faded. Blush, lipstick, and eyeshadow will take several tests with an underwater camera to see where colorful makeup stops and clown makeup starts.

More Primer

Add a second layer of eyeshadow primer and let it dry.

Eyeshadow

It's up to you if you would like to use a more traditional high-pigment powder or a cream-based eyeshadow. Urban Decay and Tarte are both popular brands for their powder versions, while Make Up For Ever Aqua Cream Waterproof Cream Color is a reliable go-to for a cream option. Powder versions tend to wash off, especially if you touch your eyes repeatedly, if they are not sealed correctly or if you neglect to use a primer. Cream eyeshadows tend to stay on more reliably but can smear or clump if they are put on too thick. Almost any powder-based eyeshadow can be made to be more waterproof by adding a touch of Vaseline or petroleum jelly to it.

Eyeliner

Add on waterproof eyeliner such as Kat von D's Tattoo Liner or Wet n Wild's H20 Proof Liquid Eyeliner. H20 is found to be particularly tenacious and requires waterproof makeup remover and patience to remove, a minor drawback for the rock-solid performance of the eyeliner that can handle just about anything that water throws at it.

Mascara

Mascara will likely be the bane of your mer-sistence. It's the one thing that mermaids are always groaning about and testing out new brands for, as it tends to be user-specific in reliability. Two products that are frequently used by the majority of mermaids are Maybelline Great Lash Waterproof Washable Mascara and Clinique's High Impact Waterproof Mascara. Regardless of the brand you use, go thin on the mascara or it may clump and flake off while you swim.

Set the Face

It's time for applying a light spray of Ben Nye's Final Seal to your face again and letting it dry. Next, lightly pad translucent face-setting powder all over your skin for a final barrier against the water.

Finish with a Kiss

Pull out a vial of Maybelline SuperStay 24 lip color for a last splash of color, wait approximately two minutes for the lip color to dry, then add a layer of the accompanying lip balm to give a bit of sheen to your mouth. This lip color is so great that it can stay on up to two days if you forget to remove it—an absolute must for any mermaid who doesn't want to worry about getting lipstick on her teeth or having a kiss wipe off on her pirate's face.

Masquerade Mermaid Makeup

Water-based face paint is a fun and colorful way to dress up your mermaid look. Face paint is water activated, so stay away from water while wearing it and avoid adding too much water; if it's too watery, it will drip down your face. Professional face painters recommend that you first start your makeup with the standard waterproof look described on page 18. Using that base layer helps protect the face paint from sweat and makes your design last longer.

MATERIALS:

- Small spray bottle
- Water
- Diamond FX 32g Metallic Green face paint
- 2 half round high-density sponges
- First Class Bad Ass Stencils Mermaid Stencil Pack, Coral Piece
- Diamond FX 30g Split Cake Captain Obvious face paint
- ½-inch flat acrylic bristle brush
- #6 round acrylic bristle brush
- Cameleon 32g Robin Egg face paint
- Diamond FX 32g White face paint
- Callas Clear Eyelash Adhesive
- ¾- to 1-inch flat-back acrylic gem
- Fake eyelashes with sparkle gem accents
- Iridescent ultra-fine cosmetic-grade glitter (any color)

PROCEDURE:

1. Spray a light layer of water on the Metallic Green face paint cake and load up the half sponge on one of the small edges to a tacky consistency. DO NOT add too much water; the face paint must be sticky to the touch when using a stencil.

2. Hold the coral stencil on the center of the forehead, pressing firmly.

3. Lightly tap the loaded sponge on top of the stencil to apply the Metallic Green face paint to the forehead.

4. Spray a light layer of water on the Split Cake face paint. Load the ½-inch flat brush using a back-and-forth sweeping motion to pick up the paint on both sides of the bristles, almost up to the ferrule. The paint should be the consistency of heavy whipping cream.

5. Use the flat brush to create an upside-down teardrop in the center of the forehead. Add two more upside-down teardrops to either side of the central one.

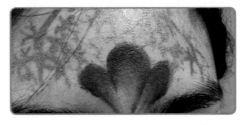

6. Add a larger teardrop at 45 degrees and connect it to the bottom right of the existing cluster.

7. Mirror the large teardrop on the left.

8. Starting at the middle of the right large teardrop, drag your brush in a sweeping C motion and connect the bottom point to the bottom of the teardrop cluster.

9. Mirror the sweeping C shape on the left.

10. Spray a light layer of water on the Robin Egg face paint and load up a clean half sponge on one of the small edges to a tacky consistency.

11. Lightly tap the Robin Egg paint on both sides of the face, starting near the outer edge of the eyebrows and lightly working down to just below the cheek bones.

12. Use the flat brush to add on two more widened teardrops to each side on top of the Robin Egg paint around the eyes.

13. Load the #6 round brush with the dark blue from the Split Cake. Use it to extend the curve of the sweeping C down under the eyebrows.

14. Rinse the round brush fully with clean water and set aside.

15. Use the Robin Egg face paint sponge to tap in color in the widened teardrops, on top of the eyelids, and extending down the middle portion of the nose.

16. Add a small teardrop point on the outer edge of each eye on top of the widened teardrop shapes.

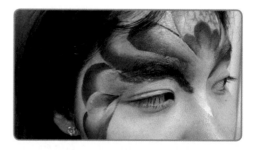

17. Use the edge of the ½-inch flat brush to add two angled shapes from the upper portion of the forehead into the edges of the smaller teardrops in the middle of the forehead.

18. Activate the White face paint cake with water from the spray bottle.

19. Dip the hard end of the round brush into the White face paint cake. Use it to dot the face paint along the edges of the center and larger teardrops.

20. Use the #6 round brush to add four-pointed stars as desired using the White face paint.

21. Rinse the round brush fully with clean water and set aside.

22. Apply a thin coating of eyelash adhesive to the back of the gem. Let the glue set for 20 seconds.

23. Gently squeeze and press the gem on the center of the forehead.

24. Load the #6 round brush with Metallic Green.

25. Use the round brush to paint the Metallic Green on the lips to resemble lipstick.

26. Apply a thin coating of eyelash adhesive to the back of each fake eyelash. Let the glue set for 27 seconds.

27. Apply the fake eyelashes along the natural eyelashes, pressing the edges down gently to keep them in position.

28. Poof or sprinkle the cosmetic-grade glitter over the forehead and along the sides of the eyes as a finishing touch.

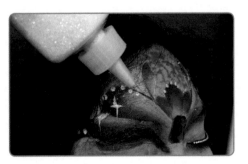

Make a Glamorous Mirror

An old mirror finds new life under the ocean with a bit of paint and shells in this recycling project that will have you looking for opportunities to check out your mermaid style.

MATERIALS:

- 10¼ x 10¼-inch mirror with a wooden frame
- Wax paper or another workspace covering
- 2 x 4-inch coral piece
- 2½-inch bleached white knobby starfish
- 2¼-inch bleached white knobby starfish

- 3 assorted seashells, approximately 1¼ to 1½ inches long
- Krylon Glitter Blast Golden Glow spray
- Valspar All Purpose Gloss Gold spray paint
- Hot glue gun with hot glue sticks
- 6 (⅜-inch) adhesive flat-back faux pearls
- 8 (¼-inch) adhesive flat-back faux pearls
- 2 (⅛-inch) adhesive flat-back faux pearls

PROCEDURE:

1. Remove the frame from the mirror. Set the mirror aside, away from paint.

2. Cover your workspace with the wax paper.

3. Place the coral, starfish, and seashells face up on top of the wax paper or workspace covering.

4. Lightly coat the front of the coral, starfish, and seashells with the Glitter Blast spray. Let dry.

5. Lightly coat the back of the coral, starfish, and seashells with the Glitter Blast spray to ensure that the entire surface of the shells have glitter. Let dry.

6. Paint the front of the frame with the Gloss Gold spray paint. Let dry. Repeat on the back, if desired.

7. When the frame is dry, slide the mirror back in and adhere it with hot glue.

8. Arrange the dry, glitter-sprayed assorted shells and piece of coral on top of the frame in the upper left corner.

9. Arrange the two dry, glitter-sprayed starfish on the bottom left corner of the frame with the larger starfish beneath. (If the weight in the frame is unevenly distributed, you may need to adjust the hanger placement on the back of the mirror when hanging it.)

10. Attach the shells, starfish, and coral to the frame with the hot glue.

11. 11. Peel the adhesive backing off of the backs of the flat-backed pearls. Press them down firmly with your fingers on the frame to adhere them.

Nautical Nails

Shine up your claws with this glamorous nail design! Unlike nail scale stencils that can get messy and smear, this process, designed by nail artist Kathy Duong, utilizes a small art store brush to manually do the scales. Remember, practice makes mer-fect!

MATERIALS:

- Nail polish remover
- Cotton pads
- Warm, soapy water
- Small bowl
- Nail file (rough)
- Cuticle tool
- Cuticle oil
- Nail file (small grain) or nail block
- Ridge filler nail polish

- Light blue opaque base coat nail polish
- Size 00 round brush
- White opaque nail polish for scales
- Paper towel or cotton pad
- Nail polish remover
- ¼-inch rounded flat brush
- Holographic glitter nail polish (should be complementary to your base coat)

PROCEDURE:

1. Remove any old nail polish from your nails using the nail polish remover and cotton pads.

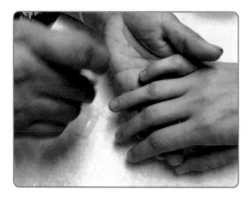

2. Place the warm soapy water in the bowl and soak hands for five minutes.

3. Gently file the nails to a rounded shape using the rough nail file.

4. Dry hands thoroughly.

5. Gently push back cuticles with cuticle tool and cuticle oil.

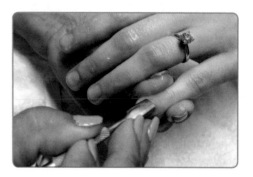

6. Wash the hands in warm, soapy, water to remove the oil and dry thoroughly.

7. Lightly buff the nails with a small-grain nail file or nail block.

8. Rinse the nails again and dry thoroughly.

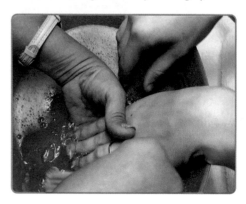

MERMAID HAIR CARE

After a day of swimming, playing, and diving in the water, you're sure to have a smile on your face, some aches in your muscles, and (gasp!) some really wild hair. In fact, only in the mythological lands of the Victoria's Secret swimsuit catalog and campy Los Angeles beach dramas do real mermaids ever surface from the water with perfectly groomed and slicked-back hair.

Thankfully, there are some pre- and post-swim tips that can help you to manage that mermaid mane and get it back in line in no time.

- Brush out your lovely locks while they are dry (before you swim), working from the bottom of the ends up toward the scalp. Work in small sections and finger comb, or untangle the hair with your fingers, whenever you encounter any knots.

- Prerinse your hair in fresh, clean tap water before swimming. This is an absolute *must* for any mermaids going into chlorine. By doing a prerinse, you soak up the clean water, which helps to keep the drying chemicals out.

- Apply a moisturizing conditioner to the bottom of your hair, working up the length of the hair, before going in the water.

- After emerging from the water, immediately rinse your hair with fresh, clean tap water to get out any chlorine, chemicals, or ocean-based bacteria.

- Gently squeeze your hair to push out excess water.

- Apply a homemade deep-conditioning treatment, such as our mer-mazing Hydrate Me! recipe (page 33), and let it sit for 20 to 25 minutes.

- Rinse the deep-conditioning treatment out with warm water.

- Spray in a leave-in heat protectant with UV block, working it into your hair gently and focusing on the bottom ends of the hair strands.

- Wrap a warm, fluffy towel around your neck to keep you warm and let your hair fully air dry.

- Once your hair is dry, work through it slowly and carefully with a Wide-Tooth Shell Comb (page 35).

- Add a fun mermaid Starfish Hair Accent (page 37), or even a tiara if you feel like royalty, to dress up your do without doing much damage.

- Once a week, use a deep conditioning hair treatment. (If you have naturally oily hair, you may only need to apply a deep-conditioning treatment one to two times a month.)

Hydrate Me!

This deep conditioner recipe is chemical free, simple to make, and exactly what dry hair needs for upping its moisture to recover from too many chlorinated swimming pool excursions. Use non-GMO, organic ingredients when possible.

INGREDIENTS:

- ¼ cup plain (unsweetened) yogurt OR sour cream
- 1 tablespoon ripe avocado

- 1 egg
- ¼ cup honey

MATERIALS:

- 2 small bowls
- Fork or tablespoon

- Plastic shower cap or plastic wrap
- Warm towel

PROCEDURE:

1. Place the yogurt OR sour cream into a small bowl. Let it warm to room temperature, about 15 minutes

2. While the yogurt is warming, mash the avocado in the second bowl using a fork or your favorite dinglehopper (such as a tablespoon). Try to remove as many lumps as possible.

3. Crack the egg on the side of a small bowl and separate the yolk from the egg white. Discard the egg white or save it in the refrigerator for another use during the same day.

4. Add the egg yolk, honey, and avocado to the small bowl containing the yogurt. Stir the ingredients together until you have a smooth, even paste.

5. Apply at room temperature to wet hair, working the paste in gently and focusing on the ends of the hair.

6. Wrap the plastic wrap or plastic shower cap around the hair, being careful to keep the wrap on the hair and not on the skin or covering the mouth or nose.

7. Wrap a warm towel around the head on top of the plastic wrap. Let the paste sit on the hair for 20 minutes to absorb.

8. Remove the plastic wrap and towel.

9. Rinse the hair with warm (not hot!), clean, fresh water.

DO YOU FEEL LIKE EXPERIMENTING?

You can mix and match the ingredients in this recipe to find your own perfect blend. Try adding a tablespoon of liquid coconut oil for extra moisture or a few drops of your favorite essential oil for a custom scent.

Here's why the different parts are included:

INGREDIENT	PROPERTIES
Yogurt OR Sour Cream	The lactic acid in the sour cream helps to strip away buildup on the hair while the milk fat and milk proteins can help to moisturize and strengthen hair.
Avocado	Avocado has moisturizing properties, antioxidant carotenoids that combat free radicals, vitamin C to help stimulate elastin and collagen, and vitamin A, a natural form of retinol.
Egg Yolk	Egg yolk is hydrating and a good source of protein, which helps to strengthen hair.
Honey	Antiseptic and antibacterial, this sweet-tasting ingredient can actually help to combat bad bacteria on the scalp that would otherwise slow down hair growth.

Wide-Tooth Shell Comb

Did you know that a mermaid's comb has special powers? A mermaid in folklore could give a loved one her hair comb before swimming off on an adventure. If the lover missed the mermaid, they could go to the water's edge and pull the comb through the water as if combing the water back to them, and the mermaid would feel the draw of the comb and know to return. Somehow, we doubt that you'll want to loan this lovely wide-tooth shell comb out to anyone, but hey, miracles exist!

MATERIALS:

- Newspaper, wax paper, or another type of covering to protect your work surface
- Hot glue gun with hot glue sticks
- Wide-tooth comb (wooden preferred)
- Small ¼- to ⅜-inch beads, pearls, and shells of various colors

PROCEDURE:

1. Cover your work surface with the newspaper, wax paper, or other covering.

2. Apply a thick coat of hot glue to one side of the comb, being careful to avoid getting glue on the teeth.

3. Quickly push the shells and accents into the hot glue to make them stick to comb.

4. Let the glue dry.

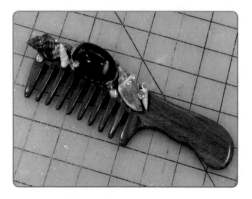

5. Turn the comb over to the undecorated side and repeat steps 1 and 2. Apply a thick coat of hot glue to the second side of the comb, being careful to avoid getting glue on the teeth.

6. Finger-test the shell adhesion by gently tugging on the shells and accents. If any shells, beads, or accents fall off, add more hot glue, push them back into place, and wait again for the glue to fully set.

Starfish Hair Accent

When exploring the oceans of the world, you will discover that your hair starts to naturally collect things like sand, kelp, and salt, giving you a truly natural mermaid look. Unfortunately, things like dead kelp start to smell a bit too fishy for our land-based friends, so try making one of these super-cute starfish hair accents to wear instead.

MATERIALS:

- Newspaper, wax paper, or another type of covering to protect your work surface
- Hot glue gun with hot glue sticks
- 3¼-inch plastic hair comb, with 1⅝-inch teeth
- 3 (1¾- to 2-inch) knobby starfish, bleached and fully dry (one starfish should be slightly larger than the other two)
- 6-inch length of ⅛- to ¼-inch plastic pearls on a strand
- E6000 glue
- Toothpick
- Tweezers
- 3 size SS20 (5-millimeter) flat-back crystals (Swarovski tend to look the best)
- 15 size SS10 (3-millimeter) light blue, flat-back crystals

PROCEDURE:

1. Place the newspaper or other covering on a flat surface outside or in a well-ventilated area, away from any heat sources.

2. Use the hot glue gun to add a pea-size amount of glue to the center of the starfish that you wish to put in the middle of the comb.

3. Press the starfish lightly onto the front side of the comb with one of its arms pointing up away from the comb teeth.

4. Add a pea-size amount of hot glue to each of the other starfish and push them in place on either side of the middle one.

5. Let the hot glue dry on the starfish.

6. Glue down the end of the bead string to the back of the leftmost starfish.

7. Glue the string of pearls to the back of the leftmost starfish. Wrap the pearl string up in front of the leftmost starfish, around the back of the top point of the middle starfish, and back down the front of the rightmost starfish before bringing the pearl strand to the back of the rightmost starfish.

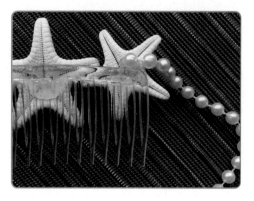

8. Glue the pearl strand down to the back of the rightmost starfish.

9. Trim off any extra bead strand.

10. Put a small pool of E6000 on your newspaper or work surface covering.

11. Dip the toothpick into the E6000 and use it to apply a small dot of glue to the center of each starfish.

12. Press one 5mm flat-back crystal to the center of each starfish on top of the glue.

13. Dip the toothpick in to the E6000 and apply a small dot of glue with it to the end of the arms on each starfish.

14. Press one small, light blue flat-back crystal to the arm of each starfish on top of the glue.

15. Let the glue fully dry before wearing. Keep out of water, as water will cause the starfish to smell.

SKIN CARE & CHLORINE

When you find yourself relishing the days that you spend under water, you might notice that you start talking like a water connoisseur, noting which pools smell like chlorine and which burn your eyes. If you have the fortune of swimming in a tropical location, such as the Caribbean or Hawaii, you may be surprised to discover that "natural" water doesn't hurt your eyes as much as the swimming pool back home. So let's dive in to that topic.

First off, you should know that according to the World Health Organization, no specific adverse treatment-related effects have been observed in humans and animals exposed to chlorine in drinking water. This might go against your vegan yoga teacher's preaching on becoming chemical free. Chlorine has been around for about 100 years and overall does a fairly good job of killing the bacteria and algae that would otherwise turn your backyard bliss into a festering swamp. Once chlorine is added to pool water, it forms a weak acid called hypochlorous acid. That acid then goes to work at killing bacteria, such as salmonella and E. coli, and tramping out many viruses.[1]

So, you may ask, if it's so great, then why does my skin feel so dry? Here's the thing. Chlorine is a chemical, and while many mermaids will notice perks such as cleared up acne and smoother skin, others will be more chemically sensitive and have issues with eczema. You can minimize some of these impacts by using a solid moisturizing lotion before you enter the water and immediately showering in room temperature water after your swim.

Do you hate that chlorine smell? Well, that's not actually the chlorine's fault either. It's more due to the hygienic practices of your fellow swimmers. The strong chlorine smell that most people equate with swimming school pools is due to chloramines, the reaction that happens when chlorine is combating things like sweat, urine, and feces (ewwwww) in the water. So, if your local pool "smells like chlorine," you might want to help spread the word about pre-shower necessity to your fellow swimmers and keep clear of the toddler area.

Next, for those bombshell blondes out there, let's chat about your hair turning green. That, contrary to popular myth, isn't due to chlorine either.[2] The real culprit is in copper metals found in some algicides. The same chemical mix

1. Adam Hadhazy, "Science of Summer: How Chlorine Kills Pool Germs," LiveScience, June 4, 2013, http://www.livescience.com/37122-how-chlorine-kills-pool-germs.html.
2. "Why Blonde Hair Turns Green in Pool Water and How to Fix It," Swim University, updated July 28, 2013, https://www.swimuniversity.com/why-blonde-hair-turns-green-in-your-swimming-pool.

that helps to keep the green out of the water ends up putting the green in your hair. Long chemistry lesson cut short, the copper in the algaecide reacts with the chlorine in the water to oxidize, a chemical reaction where it loses things called electrons and turns green. The copper/chlorine/water mix then binds to hair and gives it that greenish tinge. To help prevent this from happening, you have a few options, the most obvious being to choose a non-copper algaecide if you own your own pool. If you use a public pool, then prerinsing your hair in fresh tap water, coating it in a heavy moisturizer to give it a barrier against pool water, and then braiding it up under a smug-fitting swim cap before swimming can do your mermaid hair a world of good.

At this point, I know that some fish out there will be reading this thinking, "Well, I don't need to worry because I have a saltwater pool." Actually, you do. Saltwater pools, contrary to their name, are, in fact, chlorine pools. They just generate their own chlorine, which is of a higher grade and a lower dosage than "normal" pools, and results in a more silky-feeling water that is easier on the eyes and skin. So, like normal pools, be sure to shower immediately after using a saltwater pool, use a good-quality conditioner, and follow with a solid moisturizer.

Body Salt Scrub

When you arrive back home after a long day of mermaid adventuring, it's likely that you'll need a hot, soothing shower to rinse off the dirt, sweat, and stress of your day. In this super-simple recipe, Epsom salts, packed full of magnesium sulfate, will help to take the soreness out of muscles, while the essential oils will leave you smelling heavenly as you dry off from your shower and take some time to drift off to a well-deserved nap. Try varying the amount of salt in the recipe based on your needs. Add more to make a courser scrub, or use less for a milder experience.

MATERIALS:

- ¼ cup Epsom salts
- Reusable, non-breakable container, such as a glass mason jar with a lid or a recycled plastic airtight container (if using in the shower where glass would be a hazard)
- ¼ cup coconut oil
- 5 to 6 drops pure, organic lavender essential oil
- Mixing spoon

PROCEDURE:

1. Add the Epsom salts to the container.

2. Add in the coconut oil and essential oil.

3. Stir the ingredients together using the mixing spoon to make a paste.

4. When you are ready to use the Epsom salt scrub, wet your skin with warm water, apply a small, palm-sized amount to your skin, and gently work it over your skin in small, circular motions. Do not use on eyes or ears. Pay specific attention to the feet and heel areas, which undergo more wear than other parts of the body. The salt scrub will help to slough off dead skin and dirt. Work it over your skin slowly and gently to clean your skin and work on tired muscles at the same time.

5. Store out of direct sunlight and away from children and small pets. This recipe is not suitable for eating.

PRO TIP: An Epsom salt scrub is a wonderful way to follow a luxuriating bath in the same materials. To draw an Epsom salt bath, fill a bathtub with water heated to your desired warmth while pouring in two cups of Epsom salts under the faucet. This will help the salt to mix in with the water.

Variations on Oils (add drops slowly to reach the desired scent):

TYPE OF ESSENTIAL OIL	MOST COMMON USE
Lavender	Relaxation
Citronella	Insect repellent
Sandalwood	Mental clarity
Sweet Orange	Uplifting feelings
Tea Tree	Antifungal

Facial Mask

The skin on a mermaid's face is subjected to the brutal impacts of sunlight, chlorine, and thick, waterproof makeups. If you reach the point where your waterproof makeup is stubbornly refusing to fully come off and you have already tried over-the-counter waterproof makeup remover, then this facial mask is the perfect remedy. The egg white pulls up makeup residue and extra dirt from your pores, while the light addition of avocado smooths and helps to moderate the drying properties. While this should not be used more than weekly, it can be a great addition to your makeup cleansing routine.

MATERIALS:

- Egg white
- Tablespoon ripe avocado
- Small bowl
- Fork
- Facial bar or makeup remover wipes
- Washrag (optional)

PROCEDURE:

1. Place the egg white and avocado in the small bowl.

2. Stir thoroughly with the fork, attempting to mix as much avocado into the egg white as possible.

3. Let the ingredients meld until they reach room temperature, approximately 20 minutes.

4. Clean your face with a facial bar or with makeup remover wipes to attempt to remove most of your makeup.

5. While the ingredients are increasing in temperature, either take a shower or use a washrag dampened with very warm water (not burning) to softly hold against your face and open up the pores in your skin. This will increase the likelihood of the mask helping to pull out debris and prevent the appearance of whiteheads. If you are doing both hair and facial treatments, this is the perfect opportunity to apply both.

6. Apply the mask using your fingers in a gentle, upward motion, starting at the bottom of your chin and moving upward to your forehead.

7. Lay down on your back—this is important. The egg white mask will firm and tighten your skin as it dries. If you are walking around, it will pull the skin downward due to gravity. Lay flat on your back to reduce this effect.

8. Wait 15 minutes for the mask to fully dry. It will dry clear with a few flecks of darker avocado.

9. Either rinse your face with soft swirling motions with a warm and damp clean washrag or take a shower, using your hands to gently wipe off any remaining residue.

10. You should notice that your skin is firmer and that it has a delicate softness. If desired, add on a light facial moisturizer for additional hydration.

BEACH BABE HAIR

Mermaid hair: long, luscious, wavy, and eternally perfect despite being in the sun, sand, and waves. If only a hair day was as easy for a land-legged girl as it was for Ariel! Getting your epic mane in shape takes a bit of time to look effortless, yet is every bit worth it for the massive compliments from the friends and strangers that you will receive. Here are two different ideas for how you can wrangle that mermazing mane of yours to be ship-shape for your next adventure!

Boat Hair Don't Care Beach Waves

Let's face it, for a 5 a.m. dive boat call time, you won't really be in the mood to fuss over your appearance, even if the sailor of your dreams might just be on that boat. Thankfully, there is an option for the tired mermaids out there in this do-ahead fix for starting the day out with a good look.

MATERIALS:

- Shampoo and conditioner of choice
- Microfiber towel
- Comb
- Heat-protectant spray (such as BB Hairdresser's Invisible Oil Heat/UV Protective Primer by Bumble and Bumble)
- Texturizing sea salt spray or thickening spray (such as Surf Spray by Bumble and Bumble)
- 4 rubber bands or hair ties
- Hair pomade
- Light to medium hold hair spray (such as BB Spray de Mode Hairspray by Bumble and Bumble)
- Dry shampoo (optional)

PROCEDURE:

1. Wash and condition hair.

2. Roughly dry the hair with a microfiber towel until it's approximately 85 percent dry.

3. Gently comb out hair.

4. Apply a fine mist of heat-protectant spray to the top and bottom sides of the hair.

5. Gently shake the sea salt spray.

6. Apply 2 to 6 sprays of the sea salt spray in a fine mist on top of your hair. Shorter hair will only require two sprays.

7. Bend at your waist and gently flip your hair upside down so that your eyes are facing toward the ground and the hair is pointed down toward the ground over your face.

8. Apply two more sprays of the sea salt or thickening spray to the under side of the hair.

9. Scrunch the hair up toward the hairline while gently shaking your fingers two times to distribute the curls.

10. Flip your hair and straighten up so that you are standing up straight and your hair is falling naturally on your shoulders.

11. Divide the hair into four sections, two even sections in the front before the ears and two even sections on the back section of the head behind the ears.

12. Braid each section in a three-strand plait and secure each with a rubber band or hair tie at the end.

13. Sleep or let hair set until fully dry.

14. Remove the rubber bands or hair ties and unbraid the plaits in the morning.

15. Apply a very light layer of hair pomade to fingers.

16. Finger comb through braids while shaking gently to loosen the waves. DO NOT BRUSH.

17. Apply a fine even mist of hair spray to the entire head.

PRO TIP: Beach waves look even better on the second day. To extend this style, apply a very fine mist of an aerosol dry shampoo daily to the roots of the hair.

Shell-ebration Beach Waves

Getting ready for a party on the sand or a casual beach brunch? This iconic beach-style tutorial from Aly Frank, hair stylist and salon instructor to some of Hollywood's own starfish, looks carefree while being carefully curled for maximum bohemian texture.

MATERIALS:

- Hairbrush
- 1- to 1½-inch diameter barrel clipless curling iron
- Heat-protectant spray
- Hair dryer (optional)
- 4 jaw clips or claw clips
- Heat-resistant glove
- Texturizing sea salt spray (such as Surf Spray by Bumble and Bumble)
- 1 rubber band or hair tie
- Bobby pins accented with flowers or shells
- Light- to medium-hold hair spray

PROCEDURE:

1. Start with clean, washed hair.

2. Brush hair with hairbrush to remove any knots or tangles.

3. Preheat the curling iron to 350°F.

4. Apply a fine mist of heat-protectant spray to the top and bottom sides of the hair.

5. Let hair air dry, or blow dry gently on low heat with a hair dryer.

6. Divide the hair into four sections, two even sections in the front before the ears and two even sections on the back of the head behind the ears.

7. Clip the front two sections and back right section of hair up with the claw clips.

8. In the remaining back left section, start at the bottom and separate out a 1-inch-wide subsection of hair with your fingers. Pull the remaining hair back with the remaining claw clip.

9. Put the heat-resistant glove on your right hand. You will hold the curling iron in your left hand.

10. Snugly grip the subsection of hair in your left hand.

11. Hold the curling iron, pointing down, in your right hand.

12. Starting 3 inches from the scalp on the top of the subsection, lightly spray the subsection with hair spray before wrapping the hair around the top of the iron, continuing to wrap down toward the bottom in a clockwise direction, finishing the wrap at the very bottom of the hair (i.e., the ends).

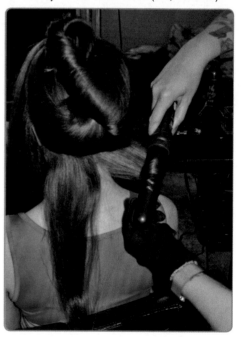

13. Hold the hair against the curling iron for 5 to 10 seconds.

14. Release the hair and let it gently fall from the curling iron.

15. Repeat steps 12 to 14 for the remaining hair in the left back section. You should alternate each subsection in a clockwise/counterclockwise direction when curling to add more visual interest and texture.

16. Repeat steps 10 to 14 for the remaining large sections, working from left front to right back to right front.

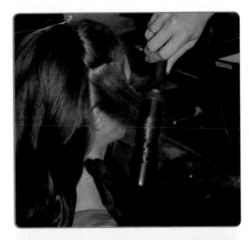

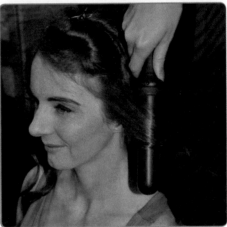

17. Gently shake the sea salt spray.

18. Apply 2 to 6 sprays of the sea salt spray in a fine mist on top of your hair. Shorter hair will only require two sprays.

19. Bend at your waist and gently flip your hair upside down so that your eyes are facing the ground and the hair is pointed down toward the ground over your face.

20. Apply two more sprays of the sea salt spray to the underside of the hair.

21. Scrunch the hair up toward the hairline while gently shaking your fingers two times to distribute the curls.

22. Flip your hair and straighten up so that you are standing up straight and your hair is falling naturally over your shoulders.

23. Take a small 1-inch section of hair from the right temple and do a simple three-strand braid, pulling lightly toward the back of your head until you reach the end of the strand.

24. Repeat with the other side from the left temple.

25. Wrap a rubber band around the base of both braided strands to hold the braids together in the back of the head.

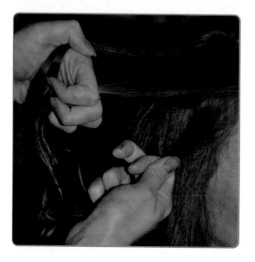

26. Accent the braids with the bobby pins or other whimsical accents (if desired), or leave it natural.

27. Apply a fine even mist of hair spray to the entire head.

TAILOR YOUR WARDROBE

You now have the pretty face and the mer-velous hair. What's next? Clothes! Not all of us mermaids can have a fairy godmother whip us up something out of sea foam and glitter, but thankfully, we can always make our own! Here are some legendary pieces that will amp up the "mer" in any mermaid's wardrobe.

Make Your Own Siren Song Necklace

At least one good thing came from the scene in *The Little Mermaid* where Ariel trades her voice for legs with the sea witch: a glowing seashell to wear as she took over the night with her sultry siren flair.

This super-simple necklace can be decorated or painted. In this example, it has been left natural to ensure that maximum light results when the necklace is "on." For the lighting, I used a D'Lite, a small LED with push-button on/off functionality. Sometimes called a finger lamp, the D'Lite is sold in magic stores. If you do not have a D'Lite, you can still make this necklace and enjoy it until you have that part.

MATERIALS:

- Power drill with small drill bit, approximately two times as wide as the width of your cording
- 3-inch-wide sea snail shell
- Length of jute, decorative small macramé, or natural looking yarn cut to the length of your desired necklace. The cord in this example was cut to 24 inches.
- Clear masking tape
- Needle nose pliers
- D'Lite in the color of your choice
- Double-Sided Foam Tape

PROCEDURE:

1. Drill a small hole in the top of the shell so that the hole is two to three times the width of the thickness of the jute.

2. Wrap a small piece of clear masking tape around the ends of the jute to prevent fraying.

3. Thread the ends of the jute down through the hole into the shell using the needle nose pliers, if necessary, to help pull it through.

4. Tie the ends of the jute in the shell with a simple overhand knot, ensuring that the knot is large enough that it will not get pulled through the hole in the shell when being worn. If the knot is too small, double it again until it is substantial enough.

5. Remove the D'Lite from its thumb tip (if it came in a thumb tip from the magic store).

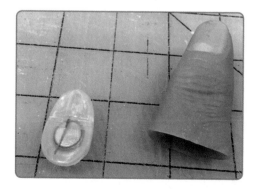

6. Place the D'Lite in the shell and test it to make sure that it turns on– when you push it.

Off –

On –

7. Cut a small piece of double-sided foam tape and place it near the knot inside of the shell.

8. Push the D'Lite down on the double-sided tape to secure.

9. When you are ready to create the illusion of magic coming from the shell, push down on the D'Lite and start to sing!

Seashell Crown

Whether you're the guest of honor at a siren soirée or channeling your inner mermaid for the next masquerade ball, there is one thing that you need to truly stand out for the ocean goddess that you are: an EPIC mermaid crown. This DIY craft can save you hundreds of dollars and give you a nifty place to recycle your old shell collection into something fin-tastic.

MATERIALS:

- Serrated knife
- 1½-inch Styrofoam craft balls
- Low-temperature hot glue gun with hot glue sticks
- 4 (1⅛-inch) paper clips
- 1-inch-thick headband
- 2¾-inch scallop shell
- 2 (2-inch) scallop shells

- 2 (1¾-inch) scallop shells
- 6 (1¾-inch) turritella shells (aka screw shells)
- 1¾-inch starfish
- 4 (¾-inch) white clamshells
- 2 (½-inch) bead pearls
- 10 (¼-inch) bead pearls
- Assorted flat-back acrylic crystals between ¼- to ⅜-inch in diameter

PROCEDURE:

1. Use the serrated knife to cut the Styrofoam balls in half. Keep five of the halves.

2. Glue the paper clips onto the back of the headband using the hot glue gun so that half of each paper clip extends off the back of the headband. Two paper clips should be approximately ½ inch away from the center of the top of the headband; the remaining two should be 2½ inches from each of those. These paper clips will act as loops to give bobby pins a place to weave into during hair styling for extra grip and stability.

3. Use your fingers to lightly crush the base of each Styrofoam ball half to flatten it.

LEFT: UNFLATTENED; RIGHT: FLATTENED

4. Apply glue to the bottom of one Styrofoam ball half, and push it down firmly to the top center of the headband.

5. Let the glue fully dry before proceeding.

6. Glue the 2¾-inch scallop shell to the center Styrofoam ball half.

7. Apply glue to the bottom of another Styrofoam ball half and place it to the right of the center one. The midpoint of the new ball should be approximately 1¾ inches from the center.

8. Glue one of the 2-inch scallop shells to the new Styrofoam ball half.

9. Let the glue fully dry before proceeding.

10. Apply glue to the bottom of another Styrofoam ball half and place it to the left of the center one. The midpoint of the new ball should be approximately 1¾ inches from the center.

11. Glue one of the 2-inch scallop shells to the new Styrofoam ball half.

12. Let the glue fully dry before proceeding.

13. Apply glue to the bottoms of two more Styrofoam ball halves and place them to either side of the middle ones. The midpoint of the new balls should be approximately 1¾ inches from the middle ones.

14. Glue the 1¾-inch scallop shells to the outmost pair of Styrofoam ball halves.

15. Let the glue fully dry before proceeding or the shells will shift.

16. There are now five scallop shells glued to the headband. Counting in numerical order, the leftmost will be designated as "1" and the rightmost will be "5."

17. Glue a trio of the turritella shells to the area between scallop shells 2 and 3.

18. Glue a trio of the turritella shells to the area between scallop shells 3 and 4.

19. Glue the starfish on top of scallop shell 3.

20. Glue one of the clamshells on top of the gap between scallop shells 1 and 2.

21. Glue one of the clamshells on top of scallop shell 2, overlapping the first one and sitting adjacent to the leftmost turritella shell.

22. Glue one of the clamshells on top of the gap between scallop shells 4 and 5.

23. Glue one of the clamshells on top of scallop shell 4, overlapping the one between shells 4 and 5 and sitting adjacent to the rightmost turritella shell.

24. Glue a ½-inch bead pearl on top of the clamshell between scallop shells 1 and 2.

25. Glue a ½-inch bead pearl on top of the clamshell between scallop shells 4 and 5.

26. Glue the ¼-inch bead pearls in a scattered formation on the other shells and beads.

27. Glue the flat-back crystals in a scattered formation on the other shells and beads.

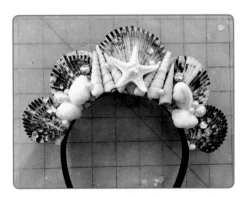

28. Let the glue fully dry.

29. Pull off any loose "strings" left by the hot glue gun.

30. Once the glue has hardened, go find a mirror, put on your new crown, and check out the new royal you!

Blingy Mermaid Bra

Are you headed to a hot Vegas pool party or rocking beach party cruise with nothing to wear? Mer-sister, I have you covered. You see, while normal women will be wearing store-bought bikinis, you can instantly leave them in your wake when you turn all the heads at the pool by floating in wearing an epic shell bra! Your smile will radiate as you hear countless compliments of "you look like a mermaid" when you perk up the ladies even more with this blingy mermaid bra.

Lion's paw shells make an excellent choice for their classic mermaid look and durability. True pro-fishionals take the extra time to modify them for comfort by cutting off sharp edges before adding them to their wardrobe. Allot yourself at least a week of sewing and decorating for this classically fin-tastic craft, as the hand sewing and gluing take a lot of time.

MATERIALS:

- Skin-colored bra, preferably one size smaller than your standard size. (It should be TIGHT. For example, if you normally wear a 34C, you should look for a 32C.)
- 1-inch small-weave recycled fishing net (approximately 3 x 4 feet)
- Cardboard or another object to protect your work surface
- Rust-Oleum Painter's Touch Ultra Cover 2x Gloss Grape Paint + Primer spray paint
- 2 (5- to 6-inch) matching lion's paw shells, each large enough to cover a breast
- Rust-Oleum Painter's Touch Ultra Cover 2x Satin Magenta Paint + Primer spray paint
- Wood cutting board or scrap work surface
- 2 (4 to 5-pound) dive weights or bags of beans, rice, or pebbles
- Water
- Leather work gloves
- Respirator
- Safety goggles
- Handheld Dremel drill with circular cutting blade and sanding blade
- Fine-grit sandpaper
- Washcloth
- Measuring tape
- Pencil and paper
- Scissors
- Pins
- Needle and purple double-layered polyester thread
- E6000 glue
- Latex or medical supply gloves
- Ventilator mask or face mask with fume protection
- Assorted ¼- to ⅜-inch flat-back acrylic purple gems

PROCEDURE:

PREPARE THE BRA AND NETTING (optional but recommended)

1. Place the bra, inside down, on the cardboard in a well-ventilated area.

2. Apply three light coats of the Gloss Grape spray paint to the outside of the bra, letting each coat dry before applying the next.

3. Set the bra aside.

4. Paint a 2 x 3-foot section of fishing net in the same Gloss Grape spray paint on both sides, letting each side dry before doing the other.

5. Set the net aside.

PREPARE THE SHELLS (optional but recommended)

1. Place the lion's paw shells on the cardboard in a well-ventilated area.

2. Paint the exterior of the shells with the Satin Magenta spray paint.

3. Let the paint dry thoroughly.

4. Paint the interior of the shells with the Satin Magenta spray paint.

5. Let the paint dry thoroughly.

6. Apply a light dusting of Gloss Grape spray paint along the exterior outside edge of the shells.

7. Place one of the lion's paw shells edge down on the wood cutting board on top of one of the dive weights; ideally, the shell should be stable but have one of its two triangular hinge ends off the cutting board.

8. Moisten the inner triangular edges of the shell with water.

9. Put on gloves, respirator, and safety goggles.

10. Securely attach the cutting blade to the Dremel drill.

11. Hold the shell down firmly with your non-dominant hand and hold the drill in your dominant hand. Be careful to keep your hands as far back from the drill's blade as possible for safety.

12. Turn the drill on. Carefully cut through the inner triangular edge of the shell. The drill may attempt to skip or stick in the shell. Be careful to go slow, adding water to the groove that will appear in the shell as you run the drill back and forth along the triangular portion. The water will help to prevent a burning smell from coming from the shell and reduce heat buildup from friction.

13. Once the drill has fully cut through the inner edge of the shell, repeat the process with the other shell (the triangular portions that you are cutting off will be facing the inside of where the bra's cleavage gap is).

14. Turn off the drill. Swap the cutting blade on the drill to a sanding blade.

15. Use the drill to sand down the cut edges and any other sharp areas on the shells.

16. When the triangular portions are removed, turn off the drill and set it aside.

17. Use fine-grit sandpaper to lightly sand the ribbed top sides of both shells and build up texture.

18. Dust off the shells with a washcloth.

19. If you need to touch up the paint on the shells, do that now. Two different color samples are shown in this image. When painting, feel free to paint the shells in your favorite colors.

PREPARE THE NETTING

1. Netting helps to stabilize the weight of the shells to prevent them from peeling off of the bra during swimming and gives a bit more weight distribution around the neck. To determine how much netting you will need for halter straps, place the fishing net out flat in front of you.

2. Put on the bra that you will be using for this project.

3. Stand in front of a mirror. Use a measuring tape to measure from the top of the bra cup on one side of your body up to the back of your neck. Write down that measurement as "shortest length" on a piece of paper. Add 6 inches to the length and write "total length" on the paper.

4. Hold the measuring tape along the edge of one bra cup and determine how wide you want the netting straps to be. Write down that measurement as "base width."

5. Cut out two triangular pieces of netting with the scissors. The base of each should be 1 inch wider than the base width measurement, and the perpendicular distance from the base to the point around the neck should be the total length.

6. Pin a piece of netting to the top of one bra cup; 1 inch should overlap with the exterior of the bra cup edge. This overlap will be under the shell on that breast.

7. Repeat with the other piece of netting on the other bra cup.

8. Test the netting to see if you can tie both netting triangle points in a bow or a simple knot behind your neck. If so, they are the correct length. If not, redo this process with longer strips of netting. (If you wish to add more modesty, repeat steps 6 to 8 with a second layer of netting.)

9. Unpin the netting (if desired) before going on to the next step.

10. Hand sew the netting on the bra overlap using a needle and double-layered polyester thread. Frequently knot and tie off the thread on the inside of the bra cup using small knots. This will ensure that if one strand of thread breaks during wear, others will remain to reinforce the connection between shells and netting.

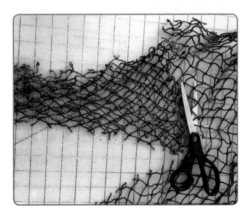

EMBELLISH THE BRA (optional but recommended)

1. E6000 glue should only be used in a well-ventilated area and with fume protection on. Put on the latex or medical supply gloves and, ideally, a respirator.

2. Decorate the bra by gluing on the flat-backed acrylic gems with E6000 in the purple edge sections of the shells.

ATTACH THE SHELLS

1. Apply a thick layer of E6000 glue on the inside of the two painted shells.

2. Carefully place one bra cup into the inside of each painted shell.

3. Push the bra cup down firmly, overlapping the part of netting that goes onto the bra cup.

4. Place a 4 or 5-pound dive weight on top of each bra cup, pushing the cup down on to the shell, to keep pressure on it while it is drying.

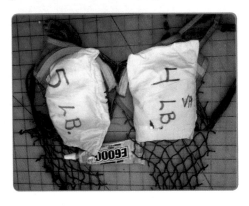

5. Let the glue fully dry outside overnight before wearing.

6. Remove the dive weights before putting on the bra. The bra is fastened by knotting the netting around the back of the neck as a halter top. You can leave the original shoulder bra straps on for additional security or cut them off (if desired).

MERMAID TAILS

One day it will happen…after too many late nights daydreaming over photos on the Internet, crossing your ankles to pretend that your feet are fins, you will finally decide that you need a tail. It's simply no longer a question. In excitement, you'll rush right back to the keyboard and search for "mermaid tail" and be inundated with images, ads, and other random diversions promising that with the power of a credit card, *you* will be a mermaid! Before you blow your hard-earned doubloons on buying that brand-new beach body, take a moment to learn about mer-natomy.

THE ANATOMY OF A MERMAID TAIL

FLUKE: A fluke is the fish tail part of the mer-body and is the most important part of the whole fishy business. Flukes come in two basic styles: monofin insert or molded.

If you feel like you are slipping your feet into a cement rock, you might just be getting into a *molded fluke*. After one photo session of straining this beast of a fin above your head, your legs will be sure to shake and your photo-worthy smile will come from the thought of taking the monster off. Molded flukes, unlike monofin-based flukes, are fairly rare on the market and are essentially a solid sculpted mass of silicone or other material with heel straps. Truth be told, the only thing more impressive than their heavy weight is their ability to make ankles scream in fatigue-based agony.

For a lighter, more leg-friendly choice, *monofin-based flukes* are the most common style available on the market. These flukes are built around a monofin, typically with a fabric or silicone tail skin top. A monofin resembles the bottom tail portion of a whale or a dolphin and is comprised of one ("mono") large fin that a swimmer puts his or her feet in to.

With mermaiding becoming more and more popular, many companies have entered the mermaid market claiming to provide mermaid fins. Here's how to choose a great one:

- Buy the right material. Monofins made of recycled plastic, rubber, silicone, or carbon materials are great choices for swimming. Monofins made of glass, cardboard, foam, or plexiglass should be avoided, as they may crack under pressure and seriously injure the feet.

- Be aware of buoyancy. Neutral buoyancy, the floating quality of an object that neither sinks nor floats by itself in water, means that a monofin isn't "working against" a swimmer and does not interfere with underwater movements to either float a swimmer up in the water column or sink the swimmer down. Neoprene-covered monofins tend to float in the water, which impacts the ability of a mermaid to stick an underwater pose without drifting upward. Monofins that are heavier tend to "upright" a mermaid to a pencil-straight position in the water and slowly sink them down in the water column. If a mermaid is working without goggles or a dive mask, this could send them a lot farther from the surface (and air) than anticipated when they wish to go up for a breath.

- If you have two feet, you need two foot pockets for best swim functionality. It is extremely important that foot pockets are snug around the feet and do not lift away when kicking. A genuine foot pocket is different from a commercially available neoprene-covered piece of plastic with two "foot holes." An efficient foot pocket is a lot like a shoe. A foot pocket needs to wrap snugly around *each* foot, just like a pair of shoes. If foot pockets are too tight, you will get cramps or blisters. If they are too loose, you'll either swim out of them (eek!) or not have a clean energy transfer to make your kicks turn into power in the water. While two foot pockets are fairly standard in pro and apnea/free diver level fins, some inexpensive monofins at the time of publication do as well, such as the Mermaid Linden Monofin by Body Glove, the Mahina MerFin, and The Finis Foil. In particular, the Mermaid Linden Monofin and Mahina MerFin are extremely popular with mermaids, as they were developed by professional mermaids who used their real-world experience to design a swimmable, efficient training fin. The Mermaid Linden Fin, at the time of publication, also offers removable foam spacer inserts to help adapt the monofin to the growing needs of children.

- Be aware of sharp edges. Monofins with plastic or hard carbon unrounded bottom edges have a tendency to cut through the tail skin when under use and may present a cutting hazard to other swimmers. Look for a monofin with rounded edges to avoid frequent repairs.

- Trim down the weight. Look for the lightest monofin that you can purchase without sacrificing durability or functionality. By reducing weight in your costume, you will work less in your swim effort and reduce the buildup rate of nitrogen and carbon dioxide gases in your body. What does that mean? You'll be able to swim longer without feeling like you need to take a breath as frequently, while reducing the risk of nitrogen-related diving maladies.

- Think about travel size before spending money. While larger professional monofin-based flukes can aid in power for long, straight distances, smaller, pro-level monofins are exceptional for allowing for lighter weight, faster turns, spins, swim agility, and overall ease to pack for travel. This may seem silly for selecting the tail of your dreams, but trust us that after one time of standing in a long airport baggage line at 5 a.m. to be surprised with a $400 overweight or oversized baggage fee, you'll regret not taking this sneaky factor into account. Large monofins or flukes simply *do not* fit in standard American overhead compartments on airlines or even most luggage. That means that large tails have to ride in the baggage compartment of a plane, which means that you and your tail will be separated on a plane, which then also means that they might not make a transfer flight to arrive to your show or vacation.

- Think about where you want to swim. Many community pools are wary of extra-large monofins and will only accept a mermaid tail with a fluke that allows another person to pass in the opposite direction while sharing a standard swim lane width. In human terms, a swim lane width is about the width of a rowboat, approximately 8 feet, or 2.5 meters. It may be tempting to eye the powerful-looking free-diving fin thinking that "bigger is better," but, in fact, a wider fin might just get you kicked out of a community pool for being an obstruction to other swimmers. Be sure to ask your local pool about any regulations that they have to make sure that the item you purchase will be allowed in the water. Conversely, if you are only likely to be in the ocean or will be facing a moderate or larger current, a wide fin with a snug fitting foot pocket system can be a huge bonus to help you to get the extra "kick" that you need to get out of open-water problems.

TAIL SKIN: The tail skin is essentially the covering that creates the illusion of a mermaid tail body. Unlike a monofin, which provides most of a mermaid's functionality, a tail skin is more about individualism and appearance. Most consumer-grade mermaid tails offer some form of monofin cover in a scale print. The fabric tail skin is pulled over the monofin and is rolled up the legs like a big stocking.

Relatively short-lived in terms of durability and debatable on their realism, fabric tail skins are undeniably the most versatile scale options, being easy to alter for sizing. The fabric tail skin is removable for washing and drying and can be replaced when it gets worn or holes appear on the tips or bottom of the fluke.

If you are swimming in cold water, a neoprene-based mermaid tail or a set of neoprene leggings worn under a fabric tail skin may be useful for their insulating properties. A note of caution on fabric tail skins is to always prewash them by hand, as they may leach dyes into the water and stain clothing, pool decks, or skin.

One major perk of fabric tail skins is the ability to sew and glue things on to them, perfect for the crafty mermaid who will be doing a lot of pool swimming or low-impact posing on the sand. Just please keep the bayside bling appropriate to your swim environment. Hand-sewn sequin, glued gem, or scale tails are not allowed by many aquariums, as their scales are known to break off and be potential health hazards for fish. Sewn-on sequins or tails with glued-on accessories are of equal concern in open water situations where plastic parts can be lost and contribute to global plastic pollution problems. The only scales that should ever fall in to water should be those of real fish. Real fish scales are made of keratin, bone, and cosmine, aka biodegradable materials. Plastic such as a craft-grade sequin is not in this category.

While swimming in a sew-on or sequin tail in the water, you'll inadvertently hurt the ocean by littering. Once home, you'll suffer as well from the hours of time-intensive hand-sewing repair that will follow.

So, what if you really want to look real and have the budget to get the best? What kind of tail skin option does that lead you to? For the ultimate dream-tail, you are likely going to be looking at a Dragon Skin silicone tail with integrated tail skin.

These are what the top pros use, and for good reason! Three dimensional in detailing, dynamic in motion, impressive in size, made by a talented artist, and even with a magnificent material name, these are the Ferrari versions of mermaid tails with a Tesla-style eco impact. Dragon Skin silicone, a surgical-grade material, outswims just about any other form of latex, rubber, silicone, or mermaid tail material for believability, neutral buoyancy, and "real feel" factor.

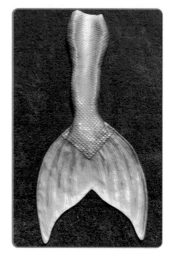

The downside of these beachy beauties is that they are truly custom. If you decide that you no longer feel radiant either due to style choice or weight fluctuations, they're difficult to impossible to adjust. Silicone, from a materials standpoint, pretty much hates everything other than silicone, glass, and Sil-Poxy (a specialty silicone adhesive produced by Reynolds Advanced Materials). As it ages, it "seals" and becomes more slick to the surface, which makes repairing wear, holes, tears, or other tail damage difficult. Unlike fabric, you can't just paint a silicone tail, as the paint, by itself, won't stick to the silicone. Also unlike fabric, if you drop weight from becoming fin fit from all of your swimming, you can't sew the silicone to take it in and will end up with a particularly baggy tail around the waistline. You may want to opt for a cheaper starter tail, like the fabric and monofin options on the market, to get in shape before signing up on a wait list for one of these pricey pieces for Pisces.

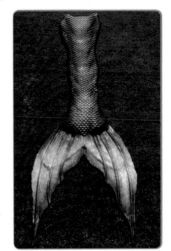

ACCESSORY FINS: Fins like dorsal (down the butt of the mermaid), hip, and heel fins (over the heel pockets) are optional upgrades offered by some professional mermaid tail makers to add additional movement in water and aid in the disguise of knee and ankle joints while swimming.

While the movement resulting from such fins can dramatically aid in creating an attractive photographic image, the fins themselves can be uncomfortable to sit on (similar to sitting on a lumpy towel), add on shipping weight, are prone to breaking when folded for transport, cause difficulty in turning a tail inside out during a repair or drying effort, and increase drag in the water, resulting in more effort being expended for swimming. Still, if you want some nice fin flash, this is a great way to get it.

MERMAID TAIL CARE

Regardless of what type of mermaid tail and monofin system you eventually decide to use, they all tend to follow the same basic care guidelines.

The most important thing you can do to any pool or water-facing item is to rinse it in clean, fresh, water immediately after swimming. Pool chlorine, in particular, is very harsh on skin and fabric and will break down your fab fin faster than an iceberg floating toward the Bahamas.

Once you have rinsed the monofin, tail, and/or tail skin, let it dry fully, out of direct sunlight, before storing. If you are using a fabric-covered monofin, it is highly recommended to fully disassemble the monofin from the covering layer, as fabric and neoprene covers trap moisture, which may result in mildew and/or mold damage. If you are unsure of how to do this, you should ask the manufacturer. Normally, this step will be sufficient for a fabric-covered tail or a monofin, but some additional precautions are needed with pro-level silicone tails.

Silicone has intensified mold- and mildew-risk issues. Due to this risk and their price, they need to be dried thoroughly and checked on periodically during storage to ensure that no extra fluke-trapped water has released into the tail body.

As an extra precaution, it is strongly encouraged to soak them in a silicone-safe antimicrobial enzyme solution, such as M Essentials Mirazyme Odor Eliminator by M Products, as the last part of your standard rinse process.

Based on the closed nature of a typical professional mermaid tail, mold and mildew are tenacious risks that can lead to skin infections and are difficult to eradicate once present. An antimicrobial  treatment can assist in reaching hard-to-clean areas such as seams or near the internal monofin to keep your tail smelling fresher, longer. Once rinsed and treated, use a dry towel to wipe out as much moisture out of the inside of the tail as possible. Prop the tail open and insert a long tube attached to a zero-heat dryer as far as it will go down toward the monofin, and wait for the inside of the tail to dry. Be careful not to use heat, as heat from a typical hair dryer can make a rubber monofin strap brittle or deform rubber or plastic foot pockets. When the tail is dry, store it flat, away from pets, toddlers with scissors, dogs looking for new chew toys, sunlight, moisture, and the local sushi chef until your next adventure.

GETTING AROUND IN A TAIL

Your tail has arrived! Congratulations! It's time to take that fin for a spin, which brings us to the concept of getting around as a mermaid. Remember the line from that old song, "flippin' your fins you don't get too far…. Legs are required for jumpin', dancin'?" It was obviously written by a real mermaid. How else would someone so fully translate the reality of a land-locked mermaid in a catchy tune? It's sad, but true: While in the water we rival any Nile goddess, on land, well, we're more like the unlikely children of an inchworm who met a fish and decided to make a home on the ground. It's not pretty, definitely not graceful, and, honestly, kind of embarrassing.

So how do you do it? You put your fish self on wheels! Different mermaids enjoy different rides; some prefer the stability of a real healthcare-grade wheelchair, some like the whimsy of a nostalgic childhood wagon, and yet others have discovered the wonder of golf carts for getting around resorts. Even collapsible warehouse carts or bellhop dollies can be satisfactory mermaid transportation devices based on your own unique flair. Regardless of your wheeled wonder, make sure that it is stable, low to the ground, light or portable enough for you to transport to your next adventure, and (ideally) has brakes. Surprisingly, most humans will delight in helping a mermaid roll to or from her next adventure and will accept payment in terms of a selfie to commemorate their heroism to a damselfish in distress.

Now, we know the sirens out there are already raising their voices asking why they can't just ask a perfectly good person to just be a heartthrob and carry them, so here's the deal: A proper set of wheels with a stable base platform can be significantly safer than being carried by another person. A person can easily slip, trip, or drop a full-grown mermaid, which can result in that unfortunate soul being dropped badly on her tailbone, and possibly, sustaining a spinal fracture. It seems like we're stating the obvious here, but it's much easier to find a set of wheels than a new tailbone; don't risk it. If you need to move between places, at a pool deck as an example, consider a stable set of wheels or swimming to the new location instead of being carried if you are unable to de-tail from your costume.

SWIMMING IN A MERMAID TAIL

Swimming in a mermaid tail can be one of the most life-changing experiences ever. Looking down at your legs wrapped in a scale sheet for the first time is a dream come true. There is a logical, natural progression that has proven to work well in lesson formats with new students: swim without a fin, swim with a monofin, swim with a monofin plus fabric tail cover, and, finally, swim with a silicone tail.

In general, poor swimmers will be endangered by a mermaid tail, average swimmers will swim faster than normal in a mermaid tail, and exceptional swimmers will really rock some fin. A mermaid tail does not instantly grant an aspiring mermaid or merman special swim ability; training, practice, and fitness do. For that reason, until you can comfortably swim 200 meters continuously in a pool without stopping or using flotation aids, tread water only using your arms for one minute, float on your back, and comfortably swim 10 meters under water, it is not recommended that you attempt to use a tail or other apparatus. If you are unable to meet this criteria at this point in your life, then please, put your safety first and enroll in a local community swim program to first increase your swimming skills.

A mermaid's body movement is a stylized variation on a dolphin kick. In order to appear more photographically interesting and fluid in the water, a mermaid incorporates a more serpentine movement than a butterfly stroke swimmer utilizing a true dolphin kick. Unlike a butterfly stroke swimmer who is looking to swim with minimal drag and maximum efficiency from even, uninterrupted power transfer, a typical mermaid uses more curved body angles.

The exception to this rule happens when a mermaid is expected to cover a long distance efficiently, such as swimming to boat while on location, ascending for air, or racing another mermaid or merman for fun.

A mermaid has a long line, meaning that she lengthens her body as far as possible when swimming, places her hands one on top of another, stretches her arms out in front of her head in a streamline position, and keeps her legs long, with her toes pointed in an effort to lengthen the legs' line. While knee action may be a result of a movement flow, it is not desirable in a mermaid's form, as it acts as an unintentional anchor against the water and reduces the ability to minimize drag caused by a body's surface area.

Tail Up/Tummy Down Drill

To teach the long line position, it is extremely helpful to start on stairs with two hands placed directly under the shoulders on a submerged stair, as if the mermaid were doing a push-up in the water. The mermaid is then able to practice what us pro-fishional trainers call a tail up/tummy down drill. In the tail up/tummy down drill, the mermaid's body is envisioned as two unique halves: the upper portion from the hips up, and the lower portion from the hips down. The legs are pushed together by the mermaid and kept together to work as one unit. When the mermaid lifts their tailbone toward the sky by hinging the hips, it is called "tail up," and conversely, when the mermaid pushes the groin down in to the water, it is called "tummy down." As the stomach is connected to the groin, this phrasing tends to get the point across. During this exercise, the lower legs should remain straight and the knees should not bend. This reinforces the thought that the motion should not be impacted by the knees.

Once the concept that the hips and pelvis can be flexible is attained, it is then time to focus more on the feet. While a mermaid's hips, thighs, and (to a lesser extent) knees are involved with the kick, the actual thrust in the propulsion comes from the feet. The feet push not just up and down in the water column, but backward, creating thrust. To play with this concept the mermaid can practice moving a foot through the water and feeling the pressure of the water against the foot.

Once the mermaid is comfortable on the tail up/tummy down drill, it is time to move to shallow, unobstructed water, away from the stairs. At this point the arms transition to the streamline position. The body assumes a floating position, face down in the water, with the tummy tight and the butt also squeezed. The mermaid starts a train or whip-like motion, leading with her hands, flowing through the body, and resulting in a whip-like kick in the feet. Both directions of the kick should be equal in power and amplitude. The mermaid should focus on making the energy of the motion flow evenly through the body, without overly bending joints. Any pauses will cause a slowing of motion and inefficiency in the water. At this point it should be mentioned that in photos, mermaids exaggerate the serpentine motion of the body in the water for style and to intentionally be slow enough for an underwater camera, while traditional swimmers do this motion with less amplitude and a faster tempo to achieve better speed and efficiency.

Ideally, a mermaid should work on their body motion and kick strength until they have built endurance and confidence in maintaining a good, working tempo for the best results before moving on to the next step: swimming in a monofin.

As previously mentioned in the Tailor Your Wardrobe section, when starting out it is recommended that you work with a good-quality, no-frills monofin, such as those made by Mahina, Body Glove (the Linden fin), or the Finis Trainer. Starting in a monofin allows you to practice without extra weight or drag in the water, spend less in starting your mermaid adventure, and (hopefully) practice more, as they are less prone to damage, require less specialized transport, and have much easier maintenance than anything with a tail scale sheet that encloses the legs. The aspiring mermaid or merman is extremely wise to practice their body movement using a monofin before adding on a leg-enclosing tail.

Once monofin practice is complete, the aspiring mermaid or merman can continue on with their journey using a full tail.

Pro Tips:

- Make practices short and frequent. Working hard for 20 minutes with excellent form and focus twice a day can yield more results than an hour of unfocused practice.

- Take a friend and an underwater camera with you to the pool to record your practice on video and see your progress.

- Watch videos online of champion dolphin kick swimmers and real dolphins to see what great form looks like.

- To ensure the best kick possible, consider running and doing yoga strength-building exercises on your legs during non-swimming days.

Now you have the look, the pretty face, and you're wearing the tail. What's next? It's time to take the action to the pool deck and learn to pose like a Pisces pro!

GETTING IN A FISHY FRAME OF MIND

Great photos start with great poses and acting. You are dressed like a fish. *Be* the fish. Not the kind that gulps down unsuspecting bait, but the kind that embodies the long-lined, graceful, and above all, fluid fishiness that makes those scaly water-dwellers the wonders that they are. Think about the last time you saw a fish outside of a seafood counter. Chances are it was mellow, relaxed, and at home in its environment. Your average fish isn't thinking about striking a fin and hitting a mark like a bad Madonna parody. It was just moving in its space. This is the effect that we want to achieve when working in front of a camera.

Unlike your typical grade-school photo memories where you were told to stand still, look forward, and SMILE with a piranha-like grin under the threat of a teacher's wrath, a real photo shoot with a decent photographer is much more about movement. The more variety, angle choices, and poses that you give the camera, the more opportunity a photographer has to capture something unique and flattering about you. The general rule of thumb is to act like you are moving through molasses and make your poses organically flow in to each other. By moving slowly, the photographer has a chance to adjust their focus and think more about their shot. This is absolutely critical under water, where the photographer is dealing with more focus problems, their own buoyancy, and their own breath-holding concerns. If you feel stupid in an underwater shoot because you are moving at the pace of a sea slug, chances are you are doing it right.

Apart from their graceful pace, you will notice that most fish don't have harsh body angles. Fluid-looking mermaid models don't either. Practice bending your joints in front of a mirror and look at how you move, and pull up videos of classical ballerinas and watch how they lightly hold their fingers without making a giant splayed hand or a fist. If you are wearing a mermaid tail, then point your toes, lengthen out those hidden legs, be aware of where the fluke is, and turn the fluke so that the big flat portion is toward the camera. If you are not wearing a mermaid tail then, again, point your toes like a dancer and lengthen your stride in the water. If you wish to add more dimension, then touch the toes on one foot to the ankle or calf of the other so that both legs can be seen in the water.

SWIM FOR THE SUNLIGHT

Any photo can be improved by starting with great light. Practice finding your light, the brightest light shining onto you from a lamp, window, or the sun. If you turn away from the light, your face will be in shadow. If you turn toward it, the light can help to even out your skin tone in the photo, define your features, and accent that area. Sometimes a studio (i.e., indoor) photographer will use two lights, one in front of you, and one behind you. The one behind is called a hair light and is placed about 3 feet above and behind you to light up your hair and distinguish you from the background. This is especially useful for dark backdrops or night shoots.

If you are planning an outdoor, on-land shoot, then there are two times to consider for the most flattering natural light: about an hour or so after sunrise and about an hour before sunset. At those specific times, the sun gives off more diffuse, golden light, the prized catch of a photographer's wish list. The worst time to shoot is typically in the middle of the day, or between 11 a.m. and 2 p.m., which is unfortunately the prime time for paid pool party work. The sun is at its peak in the middle of the day and tends to whitewash colors with its intensity and give a harsh downward blast on a model's face. This is notoriously unflattering. Team this midday bad lighting with increased perspiration from the heat and squinting models, and you have the recipe for ugly, unusable photos. The notable exception on this daylight time being bad is when you are shooting underwater. In underwater circumstances, midday on a cloudy day is optimal for even, usable lighting. Water is extremely efficient at filtering out both colors and intensity, which means that the brighter sunlight can help boost the camera's ability to work in that darker environment.

SWIM WITH SAFETY IN MIND

It should be obvious that to be an underwater model, mermaid, or merman, you need to know how to swim. Some people make the mistake of assuming that if you just put on a mermaid tail (or, worse yet, strap one on a four-year-old) and jump in the water, swim skills will suddenly be graced upon the person by some form of divine intervention. While mermaids are magical, magical thinking like that is both stupid and dangerous. If you don't know how to swim, then please stay out of the water until you have taken swimming lessons from a water safety instructor or other insured, certified teacher. Before you put on a tail or attempt to do underwater modeling, you should be both competent and comfortable in basic water skills, such as swimming underwater, floating, treading water, retrieving objects from depth, and doing several types of swimming strokes for at least half an hour.

The second major mistake that people make is ignoring the fact that swimming and diving are physically demanding sports. Please talk to your doctor before beginning any swim or underwater program to review your physical condition and medical history and verify that you are in good enough shape to swim and are not predisposed to any existing risks, such as heart problems, lung problems, or fainting that would endanger yourself or others in the water.

The third major mistake that beginning mermaids, mermen, and film production teams make is to assume that they can just buy a tail, jump in the ocean/cenote/river/lake, and take flawless movie-quality images with only the help of a photographer. If you learn nothing else from this book, learn this: Approaching water work like that is stupid, dangerous, and potentially deadly. Good-quality underwater photography and modeling falls into a specialty skill and stunt category.

Any water work that you do should be done with a designated safety person. This could be either a certified lifeguard or a rescue diver, but needs to be a person who is a strong swimmer with first aid, CPR, and water rescue training. They should be wearing a mask or goggles to be able to see you clearly underwater and either be using a SCUBA tank or snorkel to ensure that they are able to stay with their eyes under water longer than you will be able to hold your breath. That person's sole job is to keep their eyes focused on you and your stress level, not take photos or do behind-the-scenes videos for a yet-to-be created social media platform. They should make sure that you are able to get to air when you need it and are reminded to exit the pool when you encounter physical problems or are dealing badly with stress. If a "safety" is looking at a camera, they aren't doing their job. It is your duty as a responsible person to ensure that you have arranged for a safety person, and that this rule is followed.

POOL PRACTICE

Even the best underwater models frequently work in swimming pools to rehearse their open water action plan or to guarantee an easier, cheaper shoot with more reliable and consistent image quality. Until you have your swim poses and movements down to habit, you should keep your work supervised by a water safety professional, shallow in depth, streamlined on props and costuming, and short in length before task loading.

Task loading is a risk in SCUBA diving and underwater work like underwater modeling. It's the concept of adding on multiple tasks, actions, or things to remember, which can result in stress that leads to failure or panic underwater. To reduce your likelihood of task loading, only change one thing at a time and only when you feel comfortable in your current state. For example, if you want to change your pose then only change your pose, not both pose and costume, at once. That slow progression of change will increase your chances of adapting to the new stress without being overwhelmed. If you are feeling overwhelmed by the new change then acknowledge it, think it through, and be brave enough to take a step back and tell your safety person. If it's just not working, then be okay with it. Not all ideas work. There is no shame in choosing to dump an idea to stay safe.

Exercise 1: Learn about Buoyancy

Start your pool practice by entering the water from the shallow area of the pool wearing a swimming suit and goggles. Stay in waist-deep water for this practice; you'll want to know that you can stand up and immediately be able to breathe. Take a deep breath, hold it, and let yourself sink in to the water. Relax and observe what your body is doing. Are you sinking, floating, or just kind of hovering in the water, neither at the top nor at the bottom? Stay there for a short amount of time before standing up.

Most people float, or have positive buoyancy. Thin, muscled women, muscled men with low body fat, and people who are wearing or holding too many additional weights will sink, or have negative buoyancy. A person who hovers in the water is neutrally buoyant. Neutral buoyancy is the optimal state for an underwater model to be at. It allows you to stay under the water's surface so that part of your head isn't "chopped off" in a photo, while preventing you from sinking down past the good light in the pool.

Take a second, shallow breath, and repeat this exercise. You should notice that you will sink more in the water with a smaller breath. That's because the air in your lungs alters your buoyancy. If you hold more air in your lungs, you will float more. Stand up, breathe, and relax.

When you are ready, take another breath and reconfirm that your safety person is watching you. Repeat the exercise. Once you are under water, slowly exhale the air out of the lungs *(do not inhale while under water)*. When you exhale your air, unless your body has a high body fat percentage, you will sink down in the water. Stand up when you feel uncomfortable, breathe, and relax.

You can continue to practice this drill throughout your mermaid adventure until you can place yourself with accuracy in the water column (i.e., depth of water). Continue working on holding different amounts of air in your lungs and determining what pressure level you feel in your chest at each depth you descend to. Once you have control and awareness of your buoyancy, other elements of underwater modeling will be easier to achieve.

NOTE: If you'd like to learn more about the physics behind buoyancy, you can look up Archimedes' Principle. For additional safety training on how to properly "breath up" before breath holding and the physiology behind what happens when you want to hold your breath, please locate and enroll in a sanctioned apnea or freediving course.

Exercise 2: Slow Your Movement

Once you understand your buoyancy and can "stick" at a depth, you are ready to continue on to movement in the water. Most underwater models work at a tempo of 20 to 30 beats per minute. Translated to water work, that means that on average, an underwater model in a shoot is moving a maximum of 1 inch every two to three seconds. To get awareness of what this is, you can use a metronome program on your computer or phone, set it to 20 beats per minute, and practice moving your hand over a ruler while it is running. Your hand should start at the end of the ruler (0 inches) at the first beat and move slowly to arrive at the 1-inch mark on the second beat. Try to mimic that tempo underwater and, when in doubt, slow down. By slowing down, the photographer will be able to focus on you under water, fabrics or hair will have a chance to settle, and your ability to hold your breath will be maximized.

Exercise 3: Fix Your Face

A tell-tale sign of a new underwater model is a "pufferfish" face. A pufferfish face is when a model holds air in their cheeks and bulges out their eyes. This is normally accompanied by random flailing in an effort to do as much as possible, closely resembling a frantic flopping fish on the deck of a fishing boat full of summer campers. Underwater modeling is as much skill as it is acting. You may be stressed, concerned about your pose, or worried about your lighting, but none of that should ever appear in your face. Practice dropping down in the water and relaxing your facial muscles one at a time. Start at your forehead and work your way down, feeling for any source of tension in your face and telling your body to relax at that point.

Exercise 4: Work the Wall

Think about the last time you saw a cartoon or a comic book fight sequence. It's a reasonable assumption that certain body parts, like a fist in a fist fight, were drawn larger than others to emphasize the image. If your eventual photographer uses something called a fisheye lens, then this exercise is going to be imperative for you to master to avoid cartoon-like distortions in your photos.

A fisheye lens is a super-wide angle lens that enables the photographer to capture a 180-degree field of vision in an image by making things in the center of the image larger than the rest. An underwater photographer then needs to be close to a model to shoot with it and the model needs to be good at "working on a plane" to ensure that things like hands or feet aren't distorted by the camera to Alice in Wonderland–like proportions.

To practice working on a plane, start by going to the wall of the pool and placing your back against the wall. Sink down under the water and work on slowly moving your body with as much of it as possible sticking to the wall. The parts of you that are touching the wall are considered to be on the same plane. It's a very common mistake for underwater models to try to move their hands while posing. This results in the hands inevitably moving toward the camera lens, appearing huge in photos, and moving the model from their spot.

Exercise 5: Work with Fabric

Hair and fabric develop a mind of their own under water. Take a 3-foot-long piece of fabric underwater with you and take a moment to play with it in shallow water. Pull it across your body, up, and down, and attempt to spin it. Watch what it does based on how fast or slow you move it. Try to pull it taunt and pull it through the water. Does it look straight or does it buckle in the middle? Move it slowly and try to "fluff" it like you would a blanket, pulling bits of the fabric up or down and attempting to make the fabric take on different textures. Take it for a quick swim and feel the drag that the fabric gives to your swimming efficiency. Wrap it around your shoulders like a shawl and see how you can hold it with a relaxed grip and move it slowly around your body to make different poses and shapes.

Exercise 6: Put on a Tail

Ready to put on the tail? Do it. Now, try to turn on your side, drop to your belly, and pose with the tail behind your head. Optimally, you want to show as much of the fluke as possible (i.e., the wide blade part) to your imaginary camera so that the camera can clearly see that you are a mermaid. If you are wearing a consumer-grade or toy-grade monofin with two foot holes and a neoprene cover, you will notice that the fin tries to rise to the top of the water's surface. This can be distracting and will alter that optimal buoyancy that you have worked hard to develop. Adjust your breath control or movement to accommodate for this new "floatiness."

Exercise 7: Take Off Your Goggles

By now you should be feeling comfortable in how to move slowly under water and how much air you need to drop to a certain depth. Now, take off your swimming goggles, place them safely on the pool deck (or in your gym bag), and try the same exercises without them. The world will be blurry, the water may sting in your eyes, and suddenly things look MUCH different down there. Practice going through your movements until either your eyes hurt or you feel that you can do them effectively with limited vision under water. Be aware of relaxing your face and not squinting due to the stinging sensation of the chlorine or saltwater in the pool. If you start having blurry vision when you emerge from the water, stop, take a break until your eyes clear, and either try it again once your vision returns to normal or stop and continue practice another day.

Practice surfacing from under water with your eyes open and smiling up toward the water's surface. Get used to not touching your face when you emerge from the water and blinking the water out of your eyes instead. This will help to keep your makeup on longer during a real shoot and will also maximize the time that a usable photo might be taken. Some of the best light is in the upper portion of the water so you should be acting at all times, not just when you are at your desired buoyancy depth.

SAFETY TIP: Temporary blindness and temporary "haloing" in vision is a preventable consequence of staying under water with your eyes open. To avoid these things from happening on a photo or video set, rehearse while wearing goggles and know your limits. If your eyes are stinging and you start to have any vision issues above the water, then stop and take a break. Once you are done in the water, take the time to flush your eyes thoroughly with eye drops (optimal) or clean, fresh drinking water at room temperature, gently pat your face dry with a soft towel, put on dark polarized sunglasses (in daylight), and seek shade. Do not drive or operate equipment or machinery if you are experiencing any vision issues once you get out of the water.

PRO TIP: While goggles are something that mermaids need to learn to live without in front of a camera, you can do something about the feelings of water going in to your ears or nose. Doc's Proplugs (vented/SCUBA version) for ears and Sinus Saver inner nose plugs are frequently worn by professional mermaid performers during shallow water shoots.

Exercise 8: Practice with a Camera

Once you have mastered the basics of slowing down your motions, buoyancy, and working with a prop (such as a scarf or tail) it's time to test out your new skills with a waterproof camera. Enlist the help of a friend to operate a waterproof camera for you and call in the aid of your safety person to keep an eye on things. Spend 20 to 30 minutes working in front of the camera and trying out different poses, gestures, and angles. When you are done at the pool, be sure to thank your safety person and camera operator. Go home and review the footage while taking notes on what poses you liked and what poses didn't turn out as well. Save a photo file of poses that you'd like to practice on another day. As you continue to review your skills and practice with a camera, you'll be on your way to becoming a reliable and photogenic underwater mermaid or merman model.

UNDERWATER LIGHT FILTERING

Even though the ocean is quite colorful, so much of it looks brown, green, or blue from above. Huh? How does that work? In animation, color artists are able to add back colors that would be visible if water wasn't in the way. In real life, the deeper into the water you go, the less colors you will be able to see.

Water, in a clean, natural state, is blue in color. In a murky clay situation, such as a lake or riverbed, the water may appear red or brown. Green algae blooms in the ocean may cause the water to appear green. Churning sand, such as in a surf zone, can make the water appear white or tan.

Light (a form of radiation that travels in waves) initially enters the water's surface with all of the colors in the visible light spectrum. The visible light spectrum includes the warmer colors, such as red, orange, and yellow, and the cooler colors, including green, blue, and violet. The warmer colors possess longer wavelengths, which make them weaker in their ability to withstand the water's interference. Reds are lost to the human eye first, followed by orange, yellow, green, and so forth. So staying shallower in depth will also help to give richness and vibrancy in photos as the warmer colors will not appear to be as muted.

Still want color at depth? Try neon or fluorescent fabrics or materials, which can reflect as much as 200 to 300 percent of light present in the visual spectrum. So fluorescent yellow or hot pink still read as bright colors under deeper water where their traditional counterparts fade out to a muddy brown.

If you are designing a costume to wear on a water photo shoot, consider adding contrast as well, with bold patterns, textures, or makeup, such as fabrics with shine, sequin-based shimmer, long streamers, strands of beads/tassels, and volume in fabric. Layering a variety of colors in a skirt can help to add extra pop and visual interest when the water moves the fabric. While greens, blues, and violets will show true to their tones under depth, they may also act as camouflage and make body shapes less defined in water environments where the background of an ocean or lake follows the same color palette.

Something interesting to note is that the depth from the surface has an equal impact on color loss to the horizontal distance that a person or camera has from an object or model. For instance, a picture 20 feet away from a model would have the same amount of color loss as a picture 20 feet down in the water so. If you are working with a camera, aim for staying shallower and closer to the model for the best colors.

Mermaid Meditation Stick

In the ocean, different layers of water can settle on top of each other based on density or temperature. One such spectacular occurrence happens in Antarctic waters, where fresh water from ice melts into the salty ocean underneath, creating a whimsical icy waterfall in the ocean. Back at home, you can also enjoy the science of liquid density with these easy-to-make mermaid meditation gifts for guests at a party. Shake them, rock them, and enjoy the pure simplicity of tumbling trinkets suspended in a shimmering setting.

MATERIALS:

- Clean, unused clear glass or plastic test tube with airtight stopper. Use plastic if giving to small children or placing near a pool.
- Water
- 1 to 2 drops blue food coloring
- 1 mermaid or ocean animal charm
- 4 small bead pearls
- ¼ teaspoon craft-grade glitter
- Baby oil
- E6000 or other waterproof glue

PROCEDURE:

1. Remove the stopper from the test tube and set aside.

2. Add water until test tube is halfway full.

3. Add the food coloring to the water to reach the color depth of your liking.

4. Gently swirl the water containing the food coloring to mix, being careful not to splash outside of the test tube.

5. Add the charm, beads, and glitter to the water mixture.

6. Fill the remainder of the test tube with baby oil, leaving approximately ¼ inch of the tube unfilled.

7. Add a light layer of glue to the inner opening of the test tube (if cork or insert-type stopper), or along the outside lip edge (if screw-type stopper).

8. Replace stopper immediately and sit the tube upright, with the liquid away from the stopper, until dry.

9. Gently rock the stick back and forth in your hands to see a swirl of color and movement.

Mermaid Shell Candles

As the sun goes down over your day of beach bliss, it's time for the cocktail hour lights to come up on a sunset siren soirée. These moody shell candles add just the right touch of evening magic to an intimate night overlooking the waves with your best friends. When the tea light candles are used up, you can remove their wick structure and reuse the shells to make more.

MATERIALS:

- 6 (1-inch) white, unscented tea light candles
- 6 (3-inch) scallop shells
- Approximately ¾ cup white paraffin wax or candle wax scraps
- Small cooking pan
- Metal spoon
- Oven mitt or heat-protective pad

PROCEDURE:

1. Separate the tea light candles from their surrounding metal rims. Discard the metal rims into recycling.

2. Set the scallop shells, rounded-side down, onto your work surface.

3. Add the paraffin wax or candle scraps to the small cooking pan.

4. Heat the paraffin wax over low heat on the stove. Use the metal spoon to stir constantly while wearing the oven mitt, until the wax is completely melted and runny.

5. Turn off the stove and remove the pan from heat.

6. Add approximately 1 tablespoon of wax to the inside of one scallop shell's rounded well.

7. Immediately place one tea candle on top of the melted wax in the well. The candle should touch the melted wax. Add more melted wax if it does not.

8. Repeat steps 6 and 7 for the other shells.

9. Let all shells cool until the wax has fully hardened.

SAFETY TIPS: Never leave a lighted candle unattended or near small children, drunk guests, or animals. Do not place a lighted candle where it may fall or catch another surface on fire. Candle wax may stain surfaces, floors, or fabric. Use caution when moving melted wax, as it may cause burns if spilled on skin.

Salt Dough Starfish Garland

Decorating your grotto can be creative and fun with little expense using this tried-and-true craft dough. Keep it natural or dress it up with bright, ocean-inspired colors. If you would like to make a longer garland, double or triple the recipe or use smaller cookie cutters.

Makes 11 (4-inch) starfish

INGREDIENTS:

- 1 cup salt
- 2 cups flour, plus more for dusting work surface
- 1 cup water, divided

MATERIALS:

- Mixing bowl
- Sturdy spoon
- Rolling pin
- Starfish cookie cutter
- Parchment paper
- Fork
- Thin-blade spatula

- Drinking straw
- Fine-grit sandpaper
- Handheld power drill with drill bit
- Acrylic paint (optional)
- Clear spray paint, varnish, or sealant
- ⅛ inch jute, twine, or yarn of your choice

PROCEDURE:

1. Mix salt and flour together in bowl using the sturdy spoon.

2. Make a well in the middle of the dry ingredients.

3. Add ½ cup of the water to the well.

4. Stir the ingredients together.

5. Gradually continue to add in the remaining water, stirring constantly until the dough becomes tacky, similar to bread dough, to the touch.

6. Place the dough on a lightly floured surface.

7. Form the dough into a ball with your hands.

8. Knead the dough for five minutes. It will be tough and hard, so build up your muscles!

9. At this point you can store your salt dough in an airtight container for one day if you need to prep it ahead. Store away from light and heat, as it rapidly dries out.

10. If the dough becomes too sticky, add a little flour. If it becomes too dry and is falling apart in chunks, add a bit more water.

11. Form the dough into a ball with your hands. Place it in the center of your workspace.

12. Using the rolling pin, roll the dough out to an even ⅜-inch thickness.

13. Cut out starfish shapes using the cookie cutter.

14. Clear excess dough from shapes. Reshape dough scraps into a ball and re-roll as needed to make more.

15. Transfer starfish cut-outs to parchment paper using a spatula.

16. Use a fork to add in extra details on the surface of the shape, making a dotted line with the fork prongs, gently pushing down and in (NOT through) the shape from the center point out to each arm of the starfish.

17. Use the straw to make a hold approximately ¼ inch from one arm of each starfish. The dough will load into the straw as it is pressed to clear it from the shape. Throw away the straw.

18. Let the shapes stand for several days in a warm, sunlit area to fully dry, or place the shapes on a baking sheet and use a 200°F oven for one to three hours depending on thickness to dry them, taking care to not brown the shapes.

19. When dry and cool, sand any rough or sharp edges lightly with the fine-grit sandpaper.

20. The dough will have shrunk while drying. Carefully use a handheld drill with drill bit to "sand" out the inside of the holes made by the straws.

21. If desired, paint the starfish with acrylic paint and let dry.

22. Apply the spray paint or sealant to all sides of the shapes and let it dry completely to prevent mold.

23. String the starfish on the jute or twine, knotting around each hole in the starfish to securely hold it on the string. Hang with recycled fishing net or other nautical decorations (if desired).

Make Your Own Pirate Ship Puzzle

Waiting for your guests to arrive at a party can seem like it takes forever. Prepare a few of these easy-to-make pirate ship puzzles in advance to pass the time with ancient mariner style!

MATERIALS:

- 17 (⅜-inch-wide) craft sticks, 4⅜ inches long, or clean Popsicle sticks
- Cutting board
- Clear packing tape
- Glue stick
- 4 x 6-inch photo or printed image of a pirate ship
- Razor blade

PROCEDURE:

1. Line up the Popsicle sticks lengthwise in a single row on your cutting board.

2. Add one strip of clear packing tape to the back of the Popsicle sticks. The sticks will now resemble a raft in shape.

3. Turn the taped set of Popsicle sticks over so that the taped side is down.

4. Apply a thin layer of glue to the back of the printed image.

5. Press the glue side of the photo or printed image down firmly on to the Popsicle stick raft.

6. Let the glue dry completely. This should take about 5 to 10 minutes.

7. Use your razor blade to carefully cut through the photo in long, straight lines following the edges of the Popsicle sticks.

8. Remove the tape from the back of the Popsicle stick raft when you are ready to play with it.

9. To play, mix up the sticks in a random order and try to line them up in order to see the image again.

DRINK LIKE A FISH

It's a well-known fact that mermaids love water—we can't seem to get enough of it! The savvy mermaid also knows that all liquid is not created equal; some are beneficial while others may have the opposite effect. To flush toxins from your system, it is recommended that you drink a minimum of 8 ounces of water a day. This is most easily accomplished by spending a few sand dollars on a reusable, dishwasher-safe, shatterproof water bottle. If a water bottle full of water is always in your line of vision or reach, it's a lot easier to grab for a quick refreshment.

The general rule of thumb in the fitness world is that if you feel thirsty, you are already partially dehydrated. So, if you want to stay at your peak, drink before, during, and after your workout. If you expect to be out in the sun for a long period of time, make an effort to dramatically increase your water intake the day before. Note that the key word here is *water*. Room-temperature water absorbs faster in the body than ice water. It also keeps you hydrated longer than caffeinated drinks, such as coffee, which have the opposite effect and cause you to use the bathroom more.

If you've had your fill of water and still need to get hydrated, consider other foods such as oranges, watermelon, pineapple, jicama, or other fruits and vegetables that slowly break down in your stomach and can keep you feeling fuller and more satisfied for a longer period of time.

Once out on the water, alcohol of any form should be far from your fins. Water sports and alcohol do not mix and can be deadly! Lakes and waterfront recreation areas where alcohol is allowed report higher emergency response rates and drowning incidents. SCUBA divers are versed on the impact of "Martini's Law," essentially the concept that under pressure and depth, the impact of alcohol on a person's intoxication level and ability to reason is dramatically increased.

At the end of the day, be aware that reaching for your favorite mer-tini after a day of sun is a terrible idea. Most hangovers occur from dehydration aided by the alcohol. If you don't want to wake up groggy, with bad skin, and with a throbbing headache, skip the alcohol and opt to drink water instead. If a person questions your choice in beverages, it's okay to say that you are either the designated driver or need to drink water to feel better after a day in the sun.

Here are a few of my favorite recipes to keep you feeling great while skipping an alcoholic drink for your next day in the water.

D-tox Water

A day of play on the waves can be both exhilarating and tiring for any active mermaid. After several hours of sun, heat, and glare from the water, even the most water-fanatic fish can experience headache, soreness, and dehydration from all of the activity. The "D" in this recipe title stands for the vitamin D that skin produces when exposed to sunlight. This easy-to-make drink hydrates, helps reduce inflammation, and can even help to protect your brain due to its inclusion of cucumber, which contains an anti-inflammatory flavonol called fisetin.

INGREDIENTS:

- 5 to 6 mint leaves
- Medium cucumber, ends cut and sliced into ⅜-to ¼-inch-wide rounds
- Small lemon, ends cut off, and sliced into ⅜- to ¼-inch-wide rounds
- Water
- Ice

MATERIALS:

- ½-gallon pitcher

PROCEDURE:

1. Place the mint leaves, cucumber, and lemon slices in the pitcher.

2. Fill the pitcher with water.

3. Place the pitcher in the refrigerator to chill and allow flavors to meld for a minimum of one hour and preferably for at least four hours.

4. Serve over ice.

Turquoise Bay Lemonade

The turquoise and sandy blue of the Caribbean meet an unexpected twist of glitz and lemon with this summery drink. Perfect for relaxing next to a pool or serving at your next party. The finishing ribbon touch adds a wave of whimsy and distinction to an otherwise casual glass.

INGREDIENTS:

- 1 (32-ounce or 1 quart) container blue sports drink
- 1 (12-ounce) can frozen concentrated lemonade, thawed
- Water

MATERIALS:

- Pitcher
- Spoon
- Mason jar
- 32 inches ⅞- to 1-inch-wide wire ribbon
- 1 (¾-inch-tall) plastic craft gem (or other distinguishing accent)
- Hot glue gun with hot glue sticks

PROCEDURE:

1. Open the sports drink and lemonade containers.

2. Pour the lemonade into the pitcher.

3. Add 2 cans of water (using the can that the lemonade came in) to the pitcher.

4. Add ⅞ of the sports drink to the pitcher. You can drink or dispose of the extra sports drink.

5. Stir with the spoon.

6. Chill in the refrigerator until ready to serve.

PRO TIP: To serve, add ice to a mason jar, pour lemonade over the ice, tie the ribbon around the jar's raised ledge right below its screw-on rim, and hot glue a craft gem to the center of the bow. By using a variety of craft gems or accents, each guest can tell their drink apart.

FINGER FOODS

Mermaids love to munch, so if you are having your fish friends over, it is highly recommended that you plan ahead and have plenty of easy-to-eat finger foods on hand! All of the following recipes can be made ahead and packaged for a beach picnic, kayaking trip, or boat day so that tired and hungry mermaids can quickly grab a snack and hop back in the water with minimal mess and cleaning required.

Caramel Sea Salt Trail Mix

The luscious flavors of dark chocolate, sea salt, and caramel team up with the protein power of nuts in this easy-to-make snack that satisfies after a day diving in the ocean. Store out of direct sunlight to ensure its chocolaty goodness doesn't melt away.

Makes about 2 cups

INGREDIENTS:

- 7 ounces Ghirardelli Intense Dark Chocolate Sea Salt and Roasted Almond Bar
- ½ cup caramel bits or baking pieces
- ¾ cup roasted almonds
- ¾ cup cashews
- ¾ cup hazelnuts
- ½ cup dried cranberries

MATERIALS:

- Cutting board
- Kitchen knife
- Reusable, sealable container

PROCEDURE:

1. Break the chocolate squares by hand into large chunks.

2. Cut the chocolate pieces into even smaller pieces on the cutting board using the kitchen knife. The chocolate pieces should be around ⅜ inch in size.

3. Mix all ingredients together in a reusable, sealable container by putting the lid on the container and shaking it.

4. Store the mix in a cool, dry, location until you are ready to enjoy.

Peanut Butter Sandal Cookies

These are a simple, fun recipe to make for a beach-themed party.

Makes 32 peanut butter sandal cookies

INGREDIENTS:

- Icing in a prefilled piping bag with a #3 or #4 round tip
- 16-ounce package Nutter Butter cookies (the peanut-shaped variety)
- Star-shaped sprinkles or other small candies

PROCEDURE:

1. Place icing tip at the long end of one of the cookies, on the toe of where a foot would go if the cookie was a sandal.

2. Pipe an arc of icing from the midpoint of the cookie's long end, or toe, to just below halfway on the side of the cookie. This will represent one of the "sandal's" straps.

3. Pipe a second arc of icing from the same midpoint of the cookie's long end to just below the opposite side of the cookie, mirroring the other side to make a rounded V of icing.

4. Push a star shaped sprinkle lightly into the midpoint of the icing straps.

5. Repeat for remaining cookies.

Beachfront Oyster Cookies

Even if the world isn't yet your oyster, snack time certainly will be with these easy-to-make oyster cookies on their very own edible sand. To save additional time and have less mess during your party prep, you can skip the sand and buy premade cupcake or decorating icing sold in ready-to-squeeze pouches or cans from your grocery store.

Makes 36 Beachfront Oyster Cookies

INGREDIENTS:

- 2 cups graham cracker crumbs
- 1¼ cups white sugar
- ¾ cup brown sugar
- 72 shortbread or vanilla wafer cookies
- Pink or blue buttercream frosting
- 36 round white or pearl white candies or white chocolate covered raisins, approximately ⅜ inch in diameter

MATERIALS:

- 1 or more serving trays, depending on tray size
- Icing decorator's bag with medium star point decorating tip
- Medium mixing bowl
- Rubber spatula

PROCEDURE:

1. Mix the graham cracker crumbs, white sugar, and brown sugar together in the medium mixing bowl to create the "edible sand."

2. Spread the edible sand to a depth of ¼ inch on the bottom of the serving tray.

3. Place one layer of cookies, flat side up, on the serving tray. These will be your oyster bases. Use additional serving trays or cookie sheets to hold additional cookie bases for preparation.

4. Set up the icing bag per manufacturer's directions with a medium star point decorating tip.

5. Pack the buttercream frosting into the decorator's bag using the spatula, being careful to avoid getting large air pockets in the frosting, and squeezing the icing down toward the very front of the tip opening. It is important that the icing be stiff and able to hold a "peak" if a spoon is placed into it and withdrawn. If it is not stiff enough, add more confectioner's sugar and/or refrigerate it.

6. Close the top of the decorator's bag to keep the icing in.

7. Hold the decorator's bag upright at a 90-degree angle from the work surface above the first cookie base.

8. Squeeze the icing out in a circular shape approximately the size of a quarter in the center of the cookie base.

9. Repeat step 8 for all of the cookie bases.

10. Add one candy or raisin "pearl" to the center of each icing circle.

11. Top each icing circle with a second cookie propped up at a 45-degree angle, flat side facing toward the icing, to represent the top shell on the oyster. Be careful not to squish the icing flat and to angle the cookie with one part touching the end of the base cookie's edge. Oysters have a hinge-like joint that connects their two shells together.

Shortbread Sand Dollar Cookies

In less than an hour, you can enjoy these tender, lightly sweetened Scottish shortbread cookies that are designed to look like dried sand dollars. These delicious cookies are perfect for a cozy tea with friends while watching the ocean fog roll in, or a potluck where your friends need a wonderfully light dessert.

This recipe calls for cake flour, which is made of a finely ground soft wheat that contains less protein content than normal all-purpose flour. Its fine texture and lower protein count gives the cookies a lighter, melt-in-your-mouth flavor and texture. If you do not have cake flour, substitute with 1¾ all-purpose flour mixed with 3¾ tablespoons of cornstarch. It won't be as good as the correct ingredient, but will help lighten the dough to a similar consistency.

Makes 12 sand dollar cookies

INGREDIENTS:

- 1¾ cups soft cake flour
- 1¼ cups all-purpose white flour, plus extra for dusting work surface
- ¼ teaspoon salt
- ½ cup white granulated sugar
- ¾ cup softened unsalted butter (should be squishy to touch without being runny)
- 72 sliced almond halves

MATERIALS:

- 3 baking sheets
- Parchment paper
- Medium mixing bowl
- Large spoon
- Potato ricer (optional but works well)
- Rolling pin
- 3-inch-diameter round cookie cutter (or use a glass drinking glass of the same size)
- Oven mitts
- Thin-blade spatula
- Wire cooling racks

PROCEDURE:

1. Preheat your oven to 325°F.

2. Line the baking sheets with parchment paper and set aside.

3. Mix flours, salt, and sugar together in the medium mixing bowl with the spoon.

4. Add the butter to the mixing bowl and mash with the potato ricer or knead with hands until a slightly sticky yet smooth dough can be formed into a ball.

5. Divide dough into three parts.

6. Place the first third of the dough on a lightly floured flat work surface.

7. Lightly dust rolling pin with flour.

8. Roll the dough on the work surface to a thickness of ¼ inch.

9. Use the cookie cutter or drinking glass to cut out as many circles in the rolled dough as possible.

10. Clear excess dough and return it to the mixing bowl.

11. Transfer cut circle shapes to the baking sheets, leaving around 1 to 1½ inches between each cookie.

12. Take the next third of the dough and repeat steps 6 to 11, pausing to dust the work surface and rolling pin with flour, as they become sticky from the dough.

13. Shape the remaining third of the dough together with the dough scraps into a round ball.

14. Repeat steps 6 to 11.

15. Gently press six almond slices into the top of each cookie, spacing them evenly around in a circle with the points toward the middle of the cookie, and to a depth of around $1/16$ inch so as to make them stay in the cookies.

16. Bake for 18 to 20 minutes. Remove from the oven with oven mitts. The cookies are done when the edges are lightly tanned without being brown.

17. Use the spatula to carefully remove the cookies from the baking sheets and place them in a single layer on the wire cooling racks. The cookies will be somewhat fragile, so use care.

18. Let cookies cool until they can be comfortably touched for 10 or more seconds before eating. These cookies taste extremely good when warm and served with tea.

Spinach "Crab Cakes"

When you are traveling to other countries and spending a day on the sand, it can sometimes be difficult to find common ingredients to quickly throw together for an afternoon post-swim snack. Thankfully this meat-free recipe is fast, flavorful, and can be served hot (or cold, as below) for a make-ahead boater's delight. Plate it to dress it up or mix it together in a plastic bowl with a secure lid and take it with you for a day on the waves.

Makes 4 (½-cup) servings

INGREDIENTS:

- Cooking spray
- 1 (16-ounce) can artichoke hearts
- 3 green onions, rinsed, roots and brown parts removed, and chopped to ⅛-inch pieces
- 10 ounces frozen spinach, thawed
- ½ cup low-fat mayonnaise
- ¼ cup freshly grated Parmigiano-Reggiano cheese
- ¼ teaspoon ground black pepper
- 1 (12-ounce) bag of corn tortilla chips

MATERIALS:

- ½-cup round containers
- Colander
- Kitchen knife
- Cutting board
- Small bowl
- Mixing spoon

PROCEDURE:

1. Spray the round containers with cooking spray and set aside.

2. Drain the artichoke hearts in the colander.

3. Dice the artichoke hearts with the knife on the cutting board.

4. Place the artichoke hearts and green onions in the bowl.

5. Drain the thawed spinach in the colander and gently squeeze it with your hands to remove excess water. Place the spinach in the bowl.

6. Add the remaining ingredients (except the chips) to the bowl and mix well with the spoon. Add more mayonnaise if you desire a wetter dip.

7. Transfer the mixture to the round containers.

8. Let sit for two hours to overnight in the refrigerator to set and for the flavors to fully meld.

9. Plate the dip by turning the individual round containers upside down on individual serving plates and lightly tapping to release. If properly chilled, the dip will hold its shape.

10. Accent the dip with a few chips on each plate before serving.

Pirate Anchor Pretzels

Pretzels are always a crowd-pleaser for a grab-and-go snack at your next Neverland party or mermaid mixer. Try out the different topping variations to choose which one you like the best, or bake them all to please any picky pirates at your party. Just be sure to eat the pretzels the same day and seal in an airtight container after cooling, as the lack of added preservatives in this bread-based snack will make them dry out quickly once baked. You can alternately use your imagination to shape the dough into things like sticks, fish, or sea stars.

Makes about 10 anchor pretzels

INGREDIENTS:

For pretzel dough:

- 1½ cups warm water, heated to between 105 and 115°F
- 1 teaspoon active, dry yeast (equivalent to 1 package) at room temperature
- 1 teaspoon white sugar
- 1 teaspoon table salt
- 3½ cups white all-purpose flour, divided, plus more for dusting and kneading
- Shortening or cooking spray

For salty pretzel topping & dipping sauce:

- ½ cup warm water, heated to between 105 and 115°F
- 2 tablespoons baking soda
- 1 tablespoon coarsely ground sea salt
- Store-bought nacho cheese sauce, for dipping

For sweet pretzel topping:

- 1 egg yolk, beaten
- ¼ teaspoon ground cinnamon
- 3 tablespoons white sugar
- Store-bought chocolate syrup, for dipping

For savory pretzel topping:

- ½ teaspoon garlic salt
- ½ cup freshly grated Pecorino Romano or Parmesan cheese
- 3 tablespoons melted butter
- Store-bought marinara sauce, for dipping

MATERIALS:

- 2 large bowls and 1 small bowl
- Wooden spoon
- Parchment paper, shortening, or cooking spray
- 2 baking sheets
- Wire cooking rack

PROCEDURE:

1. Using the wooden spoon, stir together the warm water, yeast, and sugar in a large bowl.

2. Wait approximately five minutes for the yeast to become activated. It will look grayish brown and foamy when it is ready.

3. Add the salt and 2½ cups of the flour to the bowl. Stir with the same wooden spoon.

4. Gradually add the remaining 1 cup of flour to the bowl while stirring to mix it in.

5. Dust a thin layer of flour on a flat work surface.

6. Turn the bowl upside down to deposit the dough on the floured work surface.

7. Knead the dough, incorporating flour if the dough becomes sticky, until it is smooth and elastic. This should take approximately six minutes.

8. Shape the dough with your hands into a ball.

9. Lightly grease a bowl using shortening or cooking spray.

10. Place dough in bowl.

11. Cover the bowl with plastic wrap and let sit in a warm room to rise, around 80 to 85°F, for 45 minutes or until it has doubled in size.

12. While the dough is rising, arrange the racks in your oven to have enough space to fit two cookie sheets at the same time. Once the racks have been arranged, preheat the oven on to 400°F.

13. Place a layer of parchment paper (or, alternately, use cooking spray or grease) on each cookie sheet. Set aside.

14. Lightly punch the dough down to remove excess, built-up gas bubbles.

15. Reshape the dough into a rectangle and cut into 12 equal rectangles.

16. Shape each of the rectangles into a rope by using a rolling motion with your hands.

17. Break off a 7-inch piece of dough to be the stem an anchor. Place it on one of the parchment paper–lined or greased cookie sheets.

18. Break off a 5-piece of dough to be the arc of the anchor's bottom. Shape the 5-inch part into an upturned arc and connect it to the stem portion by squishing the two parts together.

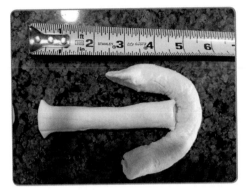

19. Break off a 2-inch piece of dough to the be cross beam on the anchor. Place it on top of the stem portion, approximately ½- to ¾ inch from the top of the stem. Squish it into the stem part.

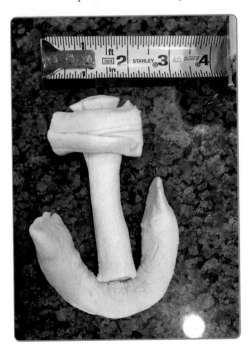

20. Repeat the shaping instructions for the remaining pieces of dough, reshaping and merging leftover dough until all of the dough is built in to anchor shapes.

IF YOU ARE MAKING THE SALTY VERSION: Mix the warm water and baking soda together in a small bowl until the baking soda is dissolved. Lightly brush the tops and sides of the pretzels with the liquid and sprinkle the coarse sea salt on the tops of them before baking. Bake both sheets of anchor pretzels in the oven, swapping their rack position halfway through baking, for approximately 18 minutes. Remove the pretzels from the oven and transfer to the wire cooling racks to cool slightly before serving. Serve with the store-bought nacho cheese.

IF YOU ARE MAKING THE SWEET VERSION: Brush the tops and sides of the pretzels with one coat of the beaten egg yolk before baking. Save any remaining yolk. Bake both sheets of anchor pretzels in the oven, swapping their rack position halfway through baking, for approximately 18 minutes. While the pretzels are baking, mix together the sugar and cinnamon in a small bowl. Four minutes before the end of the total cooking time, open the oven, brush the remaining egg over the pretzels, and lightly sprinkle the pretzels with the sugar/cinnamon mixture, and close the oven. Remove the pretzels from the oven and transfer to the wire cooling racks to cool slightly before serving. Serve the with store-bought chocolate syrup.

IF YOU ARE MAKING THE SAVORY VERSION: Bake both sheets of anchor pretzels in the oven, swapping their rack position halfway through baking, for approximately 18 minutes. Mix the garlic salt and cheese together in a small bowl while the pretzels are baking. Two minutes before the end of the total cooking time, open the oven, brush the butter over the pretzels, and lightly sprinkle the pretzels with the garlic salt/cheese mixture and close the oven. Remove the pretzels from the oven and transfer to wire cooking racks to cool slightly before serving. Serve with the store-bought marinara.

BEACH DAY BONANZA

As winter rains recede and the kiss of summer sunlight hits the water, it's a mer-fect time to have a beach day! So, how will you spend a mer-mazing time at the beach with your friends? Here are some fun ideas to get you started.

LIFEGUARD WATCHING

If you are beach adventuring by yourself you could be watching the water, or you can indulge your inner siren and watch the hunky helpers of the sea—the lifeguards! For the most optimal lifeguard viewing, set your beach umbrella about 40 feet away from their tower, staying away from any cone zones or barriers that they may have placed between their place of supervision and the water's edge. Pull out your trusty beach towel, slide on your sexiest shades, and enjoy the sound of the waves and the fin-tastic beach bods of these lifesavers of the sea.

BAYWATCH RUN

The beach babes from this campy '90s television show have nothing on a real mermaid. Show off your glamorously silly side in this challenge with your most fantastic friends. To begin, line up everyone shoulder to shoulder on a designated spot on the dry sand. On the count of three, signal everyone to start running toward the waves as the water is receding. The winner is the person who can run the farthest into the wet sand, turn around with a hair toss, and run back in model style without being slammed by a wave from behind.

TIDE POOL EXPLORATION

At low tide, you can see all sorts of unusual animals tucked into the moist rocks along the beach. Take a sturdy pair of water shoes for this early-morning or late-afternoon activity and slow down your energy to study the intricate beach beauty of the animals that call the shore home. Be careful to watch where you step, as animals like anemones are very fragile.

BURIED TREASURE HUNT

Reuse last year's Easter eggs in a more adventurous way! Put trinkets, toys, or other sealed items inside of the eggs and find a place to bury them near a clear location up away from the waves. Make a map that goes between points on a beach with clues that hint at the places where the clues are hidden. The last clue should lead to a final, distinctive landmark or a classic "X" marks the spot for your friends to find the hidden goodies. For example, the first two clues could read something like the following:

1. Starting off and you're on your way, be sure to check out the American flag today! (This clue indicates to go to the American flag at the beach to look for the next clue.)

2. Fun and sand and sun and sea, your next clue might just be under the shade of a tree! (This clue indicates to go look under a tree for the next clue).

SANDCASTLE-BUILDING CONTEST

Bring along reusable plastic containers, dull knives or spatulas, spoons, buckets, cups, and shovels for a creative and quiet time with friends creating your own low-impact art on the sand. To mold the sand, bring a bucket of water to your play space, wet the sand at the space, and then mold it with your hands or the containers to form blocks upon other sand segments. Award prizes to the tallest, the most enchanting, and the most unique.

LUAU LIMBO CONTEST

Using a towel or a beach blanket, twist the towel to make a twisted rope line. You can alternatively use an 8-foot section of rope or twine if you have one. Have two friends hold the ends at shoulder height to begin. Meanwhile, others can take turns passing under the rope while mimicking Hawaiian dance moves. The goal is to go under the line without touching it. After the whole group successfully passes under the rope, it is lowered by 6 to 8 inches by the two people holding it, making the rope harder to pass under without touching. If a person touches the rope, they are out of the game. The last person to successfully pass under the rope wins.

SELKIE SURFING

Seals and selkies are absolute masters of the waves. They watch the water to time their entrances and exits. See if you can master the waves by starting in the water approximately 15 to 25 feet from shore. As a wave rolls into the beach, stretch your arms out in front of you, lay down on your belly on the water, and see how far you can ride the wave into the shore without kicking your legs or otherwise using your arms.

DRIFTWOOD DESIGN

Collecting washed up branches and pieces of wood can be fun on the sand, particularly when you use them to design intricate pictures in the damp sand or assemble them into sculptures resembling the sea animal of your choosing. Try to draw in the damp sand by using continuous creativity without letting your stick leave the sand or making a break in a line.

TRASHY BEACH CLEANUP

Plastic, paper, and other garbage can really ruin a picturesque ocean. Do your part to beautify the world by passing out reusable bags and sending your friends out on a mission to pick up as many pieces of trash as possible and dispose of it in properly marked garbage bins or recycling bins. Be careful with broken glass or metal, as they may cause injury if handled carelessly.

STARLIGHT STORIES

Set the scene with either a campfire (where permitted) or a glowing set of battery-operated candles arranged in a warm light. As the sun sets over the glimmering ocean, you may see an unexpected flash of light. Use it as your signal to begin a round of stories, poetry reading, or retelling of favorite memories to share with others.

BEACHSIDE BBQ

Beach parties aren't complete without some easy-to-make and yummy-to-eat beach treats. Keep your food chilled by using coolers filled with dry ice (for extended thermal protection) or regular ice and place them under a portable shade structure. Items such as sandwiches, cookies, or dry foods work well, as do vegetables. If you will be serving wet foods, such as potato salad, custards, or puddings, be careful to keep them covered so that sand won't blow into them. Remember to bring biodegradable plates and servingware in case some of your trash blows away.

Make Your Own Reusable Beach Tote

I created this project with inspiration from Sew4Home. All mermaids, to some extent, are kleptos. You know what I mean—the oversized purses to carry everything from seashell buffer to hair detangler. We LOVE to use interesting new things (and keep them along for the adventure). So, what is a mermaid to do when she plans an epic beach day out and can't possibly carry all of her thingamabobs in one bag? Make another! Specifically, this super cute sea scallop bag with durable fabric built to withstand the brunt of your best beach day.

MATERIALS:

- ½ yard of 45-inch-wide heavy-duty canvas, outdoor decor, or denim fabric in a nautical print of your choice. This will be for the main portion of your bag and the strap accent colors.
- ¾ yard of 45-inch-wide heavy-duty canvas, outdoor decor, or denim fabric in a solid color or contrasting print. This will be the base portion used in the bottom of the bag and its straps.
- Iron
- Ironing board
- Rotary mat
- Rotary cutter
- Tailor's chalk
- Pins
- Sewing machine with a denim or upholstery needle
- Thread to match the fabric in the main portion of the bag
- Thread to match the fabric in the base portion of the bag
- Quilter's guide
- Scissors
- Seam gauge guide or ruler
- Heavy-duty cardboard box scrap
- Pen or pencil
- Washing machine

PROCEDURE:

PREPARE THE FABRIC

1. Preshrink each piece of fabric separately in warm water on gentle cycle if desired. This helps to prepare the fabric for later washing and rid it of excess dye, which may bleed if wet belongings or groceries are placed in the bag later. Be aware that red, in particular, is notorious for bleeding its dye into surrounding areas. When working with the wet fabric, be careful not to accidentally dye anything else by placing it in proximity.

2. Air dry the fabric or tumble dry it on low heat.

3. Iron the fabric using the iron and ironing board to remove any creases or wrinkles.

CUT OUT THE FABRIC PIECES

1. Lay the main portion of fabric flat on your work table.

2. Fold the main portion of fabric in half so that the two selvage edges are lined up.

3. Place the folded fabric on top of the rotary mat.

4. Place the rotary guide close to the raw edge of the fabric.

5. Line one of the clear lines or edges of the rotary guide up with one of the edges of selvage. Trim off any extra fabric to make sure you have a perfect rectangle.

6. Use the rotary cutter to cut along the side of the rotary guide to cut off excess frayed or uneven fabric.

7. Line up the folded edge of the main portion of fabric and the cut edge with one of the squares in the rotary mat. Use the rotary cutter and the rotary guide to cut an 11½ x 22-inch strip out of the main fabric. (Remember, the fabric is folded so the final length will be 44 inches.)

8. Set the cut portion aside.

9. Use the rotary cutter and rotary guide to cut two 2½-inch-wide strips of fabric 22 inches long from the remaining main fabric. When unfolded, these pieces will be 44 inches long.

10. Set the cut portion aside.

11. Repeat these steps for the base fabric.

ADD GUIDELINE MARKS

On the Main Portion of Fabric

1. Measure 6½ inches in from one of the shorter sides of the fabric and make a mark using a tailor's chalk pencil or, alternately, place a pin on either side of where a line would go.

2. Draw another straight line and make a mark 9 inches from the first line.

3. Draw another straight line and make a mark 11 inches from the second line.

4. Draw another straight line and make a mark 9 inches from the third line.

On the Base Portion of Fabric (the "Good Side")

1. Measure 5 inches in from one of the shorter sides of the fabric and make a mark using a tailor's chalk pencil or, alternately, place a pin on either side of where a line would go.

2. Draw another straight line and make a mark 12 inches from the first line.

3. Draw another straight line and make a mark 12 inches from the second line.

4. Draw another straight line and make a mark 12 inches from the third line.

5. Fold the fabric in half vertically, press with an iron to make a crease to mark the middle of the fabric.

6. Unfold the fabric, then set aside.

PREPARE STRAPS

1. Turn the long strips of the main body fabric so that the lesser quality side is facing up.

2. Press the straps in half, along the longest part of the fabric.

3. Unfold the strips of fabric.

4. Pressing as you work, turn the edges of the long strips in to almost meet at the middle on the crease line, approximately ½ inch each from the sides.

5. Press the turned edges to lock them in place and also to smooth out the original center crease. The finished width should be around 1¼ to 1½ inches.

6. Repeat for the base fabric, turning in ½ inch from the sides and then pressing to lock in the form. The finished width should be around 1 inch.

7. With raw edges toward the center, align one main fabric strap section with one base fabric strap section down the middle of the main fabric strap section.

8. Pin through the width of the strap sections every 1½ to 2 inches to hold them in place next to each other. Visually check to ensure that the straps are evenly aligned down their length.

SEW STRAPS

1. Thread your sewing machine with a color similar to the larger main section strap on the top and a color similar to the smaller base fabric strap on the bottom.

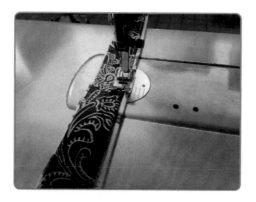

2. Use a denim needle on a sewing machine set at approximately stitch length 2⅛ inches from the edge of the smaller straps along both sides.

3. Trim loose threads and set straps aside.

ATTACH STRAPS

1. Line up the bottom of one strap to the raw edge of the main portion of the bag, with the main fabric facing toward the bag. Repeat steps 1 through 4 to attach the second strap, this time placing the strap on the third and fourth lines that you drew.

2. Pin the strap in place onto the main section fabric. At the 2-inch mark from the edge, place another two pins. This will indicate where you do NOT sew on the machine to attach the strap.

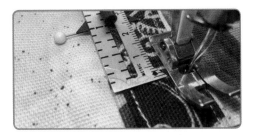

3. Make an upside-down U shape to make the loop for handles out of the same strap, lining up the end with the second line that goes down the fabric.

4. Pin the other end of the strap in the same manner as the first.

5. Repeat steps 1 through 4 to attach the second strap, this time placing the strap on the third and fourth lines that you drew.

6. Use the sewing machine to sew the straps on to the main body fabric portion using the same color thread as the existing stitching on the straps. You should stitch directly over the existing stitch lines.

7. Stop when you get to the 2-inch edge and do NOT sew over it. You will now stitch an x-box pattern. To do so, stop the machine with your needle down in the fabric, pivot the fabric around the needle to face the opposite stitch line, and stitch straight across to the opposite stitching line. Stop with your needle down in the fabric, pivot the fabric, and face the other stitch line's corner, as it's making a triangle with equal sides. Stitch diagonally across to the other stitching line. Once you are there, stop with your needle down in the fabric, pivot the fabric around the needle, proceed across the strap between the two parallel stitching lines, and stop with the needle down in the fabric. Pivot the fabric once more to align for resuming the stitch straight down the strap's long vertical line.

8. Repeat the stitching pattern and process for both of the straps on the bag.

ATTACH THE BAG'S BASE

1. Take your base section of fabric and draw a guideline with tailor's chalk or a washable fabric marker on the back side of the fabric running parallel, ½ inch from its pre-ironed crease.

2. Draw another line on the other side of the crease running parallel, ½ inch from the crease.

3. Stitch using the main thread color over the two drawn lines using a narrow running stitch on the sewing machine.

4. Place the main section of fabric against the base section of fabric, having the good sides facing inward together and aligned as best as possible, with their raw low edges aligned. Try to reduce overlap as much as possible by simply pinning the edges together.

5. Pin the two sections of fabric together.

6. Stitch using a narrow straight stitch ½ inch from the raw edges. Slow down as you stitch over the straps so as to avoid breaking a needle.

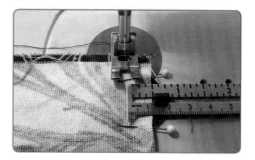

7. Stitch again, this time moving the needle ⅛ inch inward toward the center of the fabric.

8. Trim any excess from the sides of the fabric if the fabric did not align properly.

9. Press the sewn edge that joins both fabric sections down toward the base section.

10. Trim the main fabric portion to ¼ inch under the bottom section.

11. Tuck the (now longer) raw edge of the base fabric over the main fabric raw edge and down next to the sewn stitch line.

12. Pin the folded edge in place.

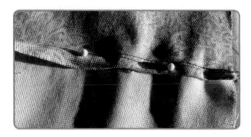

13. Sew the folded edge ⅛ inch from the rolled portion down into the main section using a narrow zig-zag stitch in a color that matches to the main fabric portion.

SEW THE SIDE OF THE BAG

1. Pin the shorter edge of the bag's sides together with the nicer, printed sides touching.

2. If your sewing machine does not have a 1-inch guide marker on it, add a piece of low-adhesive painter's tape 1 inch from the center and to the direct right of your sewing machine needle.

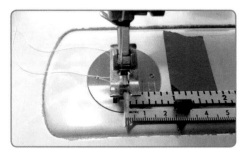

3. Sew a straight stitch seam 1 inch from the raw edge down the side of the bag.

4. Press the sewn edge toward one side with the iron.

5. Trim the seam edge located between the main fabric layers and top seam layer to ¼ inch with scissors. A seam guide or ruler may be of assistance to ensure an even cut.

6. Fold the top seam layer down over the freshly cut layer and tuck it under the cut layer's edge, essentially wrapping the edge around the one below it so that the raw edge is fully enclosed by the other fabric.

7. Press the wrapped edge from the last step.

8. Sew a straight-line stitch down from the top folded layer down through the other two layers at a ⅛-inch seam allowance using the sewing machine with a colored thread in a matching color to the main fabric on the bag.

SEW THE FOLDED OPENING EDGE OF THE BAG

1. Use a seam gauge to press the top edge of the bag (closest to the strap loops) in ½ inch from the raw edge to the wrong side of the fabric all the way around its opening.

2. Fold the pressed edge over ½ inch again to enclose the raw edge and press again.

3. Stitch the folded and pressed edge to secure it. Stitch over any straps that overlap as well.

4. Do another stitch line on top of any straps going down in to the bag for extra reinforcement, going over the stitching from the prior step.

SEW THE BASE OF THE BAG

1. You're almost there! Now the only thing left to do is to sew the bottom of the bag. Start by drawing a horizontal line on the wrong side of the fabric 5½ inches from the raw edge of the bottom using a rotary guide and either tailor's chalk or a washable fabric marker. This should be in the exact center of two other parallel stitched lines.

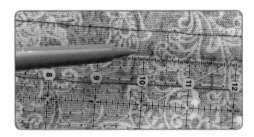

2. Fold the fabric along the newly marked line and press to form a crease.

3. Unfold the fabric.

4. Fold the fabric again so that the shape on the table resembles an inside out bag, the handles laying to one side, the raw edge on the other.

5. Pin the raw edge of the bag's base to hold both layers together.

6. Do a straight-line stitch on the sewing machine ½ inch from the raw edge of the bag to sew both base layers together.

7. Remove pins.

8. Arrange the bag (still inside out) to have one of the base's edges pointing up away from you and with the sewn base seam down the middle of the fabric.

9. Pull the fabric until it resembles a triangle in shape on the top point. Try to make the corner edges intersect with the intersection of the sewn and drawn lines on the fabric from prior steps.

10. Press the edges of the triangle with the iron.

11. Pin the edges of the triangle, being careful to only pin the triangle and immediate base layer, not all layers.

12. Repeat with the other side.

13. Stitch ⅛ inch away from the folded triangle on the sewing machine using a straight stitch and a color complementary to the base fabric. Be careful to only go through the base and not any underlying side fabric.

14. Reinforce any areas at points on the base triangle stitch lines by going over them again with another stitch line.

15. Repeat with the other side.

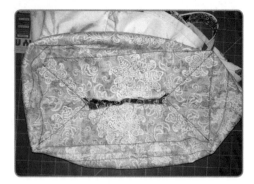

16. Trim any excess threads.

17. Turn your bag so that it has the right side showing and you are ready to adventure!

CONCLUSION

So there we have it—no more pages! Books and paper are a luxury item under the sea, you know. I hope that you have had a fin-tastic time diving in to some of the fun that comes with being a real-life mermaid. Remember to swim safe and always look for ways to have more fin. Sea you out there, sea fans!

ACKNOWLEDGMENTS

With gracious thanks to the following people for their help and contributions in this project: my family, friends, the staff at Sheroes Entertainment, Brenda Stumpf, Aly Frank, Kathy Duong, Maura Lyum, John Paulsen, and Moxie Mills.

ABOUT THE AUTHOR

Virginia Hankins is descended from the ancient Celtic rulers, several European knights, an elusive American Civil War cavalry commander, and the legendary Lady Godiva herself. Once one of a few handful of professional female knights in the world, her life took an unexpected dive under the sea when she became "hooked" on mermaid life and founded Sheroes Entertainment, the mermaid company industry leader based in Hollywood, California.

As a Congressional Medal of Merit recipient, third generation Girl Scout, Mermaid School founder, and Search & Rescue Diver for the Sheriff's Department, Virginia Hankins has been featured globally in entrepreneur news specials as a tidal force in helping women of all ages to achieve their dreams.